Tragic Comedies of Humans

Following Sophocles's
Oedipus at Colonus

Art Aeon

Tragic Comedies of Humans:
Following Sophocles's *Oedipus at Colonus*
by Art Aeon

ISBN: 9781990060007

Publisher: AEON PRESS, Halifax, NS, Canada

Printer & Distributor: Amazon. com KDP, USA

Copyright holder: Myong G. Yoon (2020)

An old version of this book was published in 2011
by Aeon Press, Canada, under the title:
Beyond the Tragedies of Oedipus and Antigone
by Art Aeon (ISBN 9780980928129).

Books of Poetry by Art Aeon

Flowing with Seasons (2003)
Hymn to Shining Mountains: the Canadian Rockies (2004)
In the Range of Light: the Yosemite (2005)
Snowflakes on Old Pines (2006)
Prayer to Sea (2007)
Echoes from Times Past (2008)
Breathing in Dao [道] (2009)
The Final Day of Socrates (2010)
Beyond the Tragedies of Oedipus and Antigone (2011)
Dù Fǔ [杜 甫] *and a Pilgrim* (2012)
The Yosemite: Images and Echoes (2013)
Revealing Dream of Vergil (2014)
Homer and Odysseus (2015)
Enigmas of the Trojan War (2016)
Beyond the Trojan War (2017)
Cycles of Seasons (2018)*
Hymn to Canadian Rockies (2019)*
Socrates with Xanthippe on his Last Day (2019)*
Dante's Poem of Light (2019)*
Journey of Life on Earth (2019)*
Mystery of the Universe (2019)*
Flowing with Seasons (2020)*
Hymn to the Range of Light (2020)*
Hymn to Sea (2020)*
Following Homer's Odyssey (2020)*
Human Causes of the Trojan War (2020)*
Awakening to One's Conscience (2020)*
Tragic Comedies of Humans (2020)*
Virgil's Last Dream of Aeneas and Homer (2020)*
Du Fu [杜 甫] *with his Last Pilgrim* (2020)*

*Printed and distributed by Amazon. com's KDP platform.

Synopsis

"Tragic Comedies of Humans:
Following Sophocles's ***Oedipus at Colonus"***
is a drama about the Greek mythological character
Oedipus in the tercet stanza. The play unfolds an
imaginary trial of Oedipus at the divine court of the
final judgment of the dead in Hades; how he is
absolved from crimes he had committed
inadvertently to avoid what the fake oracles, falsely
attributed to Apollo by his sly vile foes. Thus
acquitted, Oedipus is invited by Apollo to re-enact
his past in a play, *Tragic Comedies of Humans,* to
be performed in Olympus for the gods to watch and
appreciate. But Oedipus politely declines it as he
wishes to transcend into nobody. After Oedipus's
awe-inspiring sublime transcendence into
nothingness at peace, Apollo gives up his plan in
despair. Then Hermes offers to Apollo that he will
assume the crucial tragic role of *Oedipus* to perform
the play in Olympus.

Dedicated to

Sophocles (c. 496 – 406 BCE)

Your sublime art of tragedy
inspires me to imagine what
you left unsung in this plain play.

Tragic Comedies of Humans:

Following Sophocles's *Oedipus at Colonus*

Dramatis Personae
(in the order of their appearance)

Oedipus: the acclaimed king of Thebes
Hermes: the divine guide of the dead
Persephone: the queen of the Netherworld
Six divine judges of the final judgment of the dead
Apollo: the god of prophecy
Acastus: the Oedipus's antagonist in Corinth; father of Arete
Laius: the king of Thebes, preceding Oedipus
Thrall of Laius and Jocasta
Tiresias: the seer of Thebes
Jocasta: the queen of Laius and mother/consort of Oedipus
Antigone: the daughter of Oedipus
Arete: the Oedipus's beloved maiden in Corinth;
        the surrogate mother of Oedipus's children

Fourteen Scenes of
Tragic Comedies of Humans

< Verse Lines>

[Scene 1] *Hermes's Guidance of Oedipus's Ghost* <1-61>

[Scene 2] *Judgment of Oedipus at Divine Court* <62-243>

[Scene 3] *Fake Oracles Attributed to Apollo* <244-323>

[Scene 4] *Oedipus's Suspicion of Acastus's Plot* <324-482>

[Scene 5] *Acastus's Confession of his Hoax* <483-690>

[Scene 6] *Laius's Confession of his Infanticide* <691-749>

[Scene 7] *Testimony by Laius's Thrall* <750-1127>

[Scene 8] *Tiresias's Boast of his Divination* <1128-1305>

[Scene 9] *Jocasta's Testimony* <1306-1679>

[Scene 10] *Antigone's Sudden Appearance* <1680-1922>

[Scene 11] *Arete's Testimony* <1923-2112>

[Scene 12] *Apollo and Hermes converse
on Humanity and Divinity* <2113-2273>

[Scene 13] *Antigone Acclaimed as a Divine Judge* <2274-2361>

[Scene 14] *Departure of Oedipus into Nothingness* <2362-2439>

Scene 1

Hermes's Guidance of Oedipus's Ghost

Following the awe-inspiring death of Oedipus at Colonus [which was depicted by Sophocles (496 – 406 BCE) in his sublime tragedy: *Oedipus at Colonus*], the ghost of the self-blinded Oedipus struggles to find his way to the court of the divine judgment. He supplicates Hermes for help. In compassion, Hermes comes down and leads the helpless Oedipus to face his trial at the divine court of the final judgment.

Scene 1: *Hermes's Guidance of Oedipus's Ghost*

*{The blind ghost of Oedipus walks alone on his way
to Hades after he met his death at Colonus.}*

[Oedipus]

O awesome mystic voice,
calling me from within, whither
do you summon this miserable blind husk   3
   of accursed hapless man?
To an unknown dark realm beyond
my ken—to where should I move my blind steps?   6
   It is the vanity
of man that craves excesses in life,
inane paltry follies in empty dreams: 9
   When the blooming youth passes
with its fleeting spring, troubles on
more troubles whelm; woes on worse woes wail.   12
   And nobody can escape
the gripping harsh hands of his fate.
The longer lingers life, the heavier heave   15

 dire throes in suffering soul,
and pangs of pains in wasting body
of nobody—a fleeting shade! For those who   18
   languish on life's weary road,
one doom awaits all at the common end:
Death releases us to return to nothingness.   21

{Suddenly Oedipus stumbles and falls.
 He laments and prays.}

 Ah no more, can I move!
Help me gods; may Hermes come down
and guide me to see Queen Persephone.   24

{Lightning and thunders.
Hermes enters and gently raises Oedipus.}

[Hermes]

 Ah, the most piteous
amongst mortals, what gruesome, gory sight
you retain even after death, wretched blind   27
   ghost of proud Oedipus!
In your reckless, excessive rages,
you obliterated your own eyes beyond   30

the decree of your fate:
If a man suffered blindness by
nature, his ghost regains sight when he dies.   33
  Out of compassion, I
will guide you to reach the dark shrine
of the Queen of the dead, Persephone.   36
  You shall stand on trial
at her court of the final judgment.
Persephone is the only one who can   39
  restore your vision,
if she finds you innocent and
hence exonerates Oedipus from all wrong,   42
  false accusations from
the tumultuous world of mortals.

     [Oedipus]

O Hermes, I hear your kind divine voice,   45
  although I cannot see
your visage. I repent my rash,
violent rages that did away with my bright sight: 48

I was too fearful of
seeing my father and my mother—wife,
even in Hades. Thank you for your mercy   51
  in guiding me to reach
the realm of Queen Persephone.
I shall obey the verdict of her final   54
  judgment in humility.

        [Hermes]

Follow me, upright Oedipus.
I will lead you safely through dark passages,   57
  over mystic lands and seas,
past shadows of sunsets, and shores
of dreams, to the realm of the dead from which   60
  no one ever returns.

*{Hermes gently holds the hand of the blind, helpless
ghost of Oedipus and leads him to reach the temple
of Persephone.   The end of Scene #1.}*

Scene 2

Judgment of Oedipus at the Divine Court

Queen Persephone sits on her throne with six divine judges at the court of the final judgment of the dead in Hade. Hermes enters, leading the blind Oedipus. Persephone asks Oedipus who he was and what he did while he was alive. Oedipus confesses that unwittingly he killed his father, King Laius of Thebes, and was married to the widowed Queen Jocasta, his own mother. The appalled judges ask Oedipus why he committed such abhorred misdeeds unintendedly. Oedipus avows that the Delphic oracle of Apollo presaged that he had been so doomed even before he was conceived. The court decides to send a judge to see Apollo to confirm Oedipus's incredible claims.

[Hermes]

Hail, Queen Persephone! I bring
a new shade of man for your divine judgment.   63

[Persephone]

O Hermes, the trusty guide
from high Olympus, what urgent
matter has brought you down here to visit   66
    this gloomy realm? Do you bring
a new decree from Zeus to us?

[Hermes]

No. It is my private visit to help   69
    this forlorn hapless ghost
for compassion as he entreated
me to guide him to your court for judgment.   72

[Persephone]

Who is this disfigured
ghost? Why do you deem that he may
deserve our attention now, while countless   75
   other ghosts have been waiting
on the dismal shore of Acheron
indefinitely until Charon chooses   78
   to ferry them to reach
this court?

[Hermes]

      I shall not speak anything
about him as it falls on your jurisdiction.   81
   Ask him who he was; what
he did. If you find that he does not
deserve your attention now, dismiss him.   84
   Farewell Queen Persephone!

{Hermes leaves.}

[Persephone to Oedipus]

Who are you? Have you been blind from birth?

[Oedipus]

I am Oedipus of Thebes. I lost my sight   87
  by self-inflicted injury
to my bright eyes.

[Persephone]

          What? Why did you
inflict such cruel harm to yourself?   90

[Oedipus]

  In acute throes of shame
and agony when I found out who
I was in truth, I took out my eyeballs   93
  to punish my hateful self—
never to see anything but darkness.

[Persephone]

Who, did you find out, you were, Oedipus?   96

[Oedipus]

I realized that I was
the very killer of my sire, King
Laius of Thebes, unknown to me; much worse,   99
  that unwittingly I
had been married to his widowed
queen, Jocasta, who turned out to be none   102
  other than my own mother
who had begotten me by Laius!

[First Judge]

What? Ah how horrible to see such vile,   105
  abhorred, ghastly villain!
He should be scorched forever with
blazing fires to purge his terrible crimes.   108

[Persephone to First Judge]

Please hold your judgment yet.

Scene 2: Judgment of Oedipus at the Divine Court

[Persephone to all judges]

I would like to investigate now
the real causes of the horrible misdeeds,   111
 confessed by Oedipus,
if you all agree with me that his
perplexing case deserves our prompt attention.   114

[All six Judges]

Yes, we must probe it right away.

[Persephone]

Do you maintain, Oedipus, that
you had committed all your dreadful misdeeds   117
 without knowing what you
were doing?

[Oedipus]

         Yes, I do solemnly
avow it. Unflinchingly, I strove to avoid   120

my awful fate, only
to find out later that I had
fulfilled the dreadful prophecies.

[Persephone]

                       Prophecies?   123
What did they presage?

[Oedipus]

I had been doomed to kill my royal
father, even before I was conceived   126
   in my mother's womb; much
worse, to mate with my own mother,
begetting our children from the same womb   129
   that had brought me to this world.

[Second Judge]

What? Who did utter such awful
gruesome prophecies?

[Oedipus]

      The sacred Delphic oracle   32
of Apollo.

[Persephone]

      If so,
do you wish to plead us that you are
innocent, despite your abhorred misdeeds   135
  as you had been a hapless
victim, doomed before you were born
to carry out those awful prophecies which were   138
  somehow cursed upon you
by Apollo?

[Oedipus]

      I am guilty
for my horrible crimes as I did them   141
  with my own intention
to avoid what those terrible
oracles presaged me to do; had I   144

never heard of my dire
doom by those prophecies, I would not
kill Laius accidentally, then unknown to me   147
   that he was my father,
nor wed Jocasta—my mother,
all unwittingly at that time in eventful   150
   courses of my condemned life.

[Third Judge]

Tell us how you happened to commit
such awful misdeeds in ignorance as you   153
   claim, and how finally
you found them out with concrete proofs.

[Oedipus]

From my infancy to happy youth, I had   156
   been brought up by the king,
Polybus and his queen, Merope,
of Corinth as if I were their own beloved   159
   son and their certain heir
to succeed to the throne of Corinth.

[Fourth Judge]

How did your fortune change so drastically?   162

[Oedipus]

One day, a nobleman
of Corinth accused me as a base
foundling who would bring shameful harms   165
   and utter disasters
to Corinth. Deeply hurt in my pride,
I went to Delphi to ask of my destiny.   168
   In shock, I heard that I
had been doomed to kill my father,
and to mate with my own mother! In terrors   171
   and agonies, I fled away
from Corinth, never to see again
my revered father Polybus and my   174
   gracious mother, Merope
in my life.

[Fifth Judge]

From whom did you hear
the prophecy that such an awful doom awaited you?   177

[Oedipus]

From a priest at the Delphic
shrine of Apollo.

[Sixth Judge]

Did you ask
the priest why you had been so condemned   180
   to carry out such abhorred
horrible misdeeds?

[Oedipus]

No, I could not
dare to ask such bold question, although that is   183
   the most vital truth I
wish to know, if it is ever
possible for a mortal to learn how   186
   the gods mete out one's fate.

Scene 2: Judgment of Oedipus at the Divine Court

[Persephone]

Your perplexing case concerns with
the crucial matter on the divine justice. 189
   Do you wish to plead this court
to appeal to Apollo so that
he may reveal to us the reason why 192
   you had been foreordained
to commit such horrible crimes
ere you were conceived?

[Oedipus]

                 Of course, I do entreat 195
   you for it, if it be
ever possible!

[Persephone to the judges]

         Would you debate
on the merit of Oedipus's plea and 198
   decide on what action
we must take on.

[Second Judge]

We should ask
Apollo why Oedipus had been condemned   201
  to do such horrible
misdeeds that he strove to avoid
resolutely, if what he has attested to us   204
  is true.

[First Judge]

I disagree.
We should not intrude in secret
divine affairs about the fates of paltry   207
  mortals.

[Third Judge]

There is nothing wrong
in asking Apollo to tell us.
If he refuses, then so be it as we   210
  cannot compel him to
reveal his secret, yet we tried
to do our best.

[Fourth Judge]

    The case of Oedipus   213
 raises a vital question:
What is the divine justice? Is it
the secret whims of the Olympian gods, 216
 or the inevitable
workings of necessity?

[Fifth Judge]

By all means, we should try to find out the true 219
 nature of divine justice.
Otherwise, what are we judging
here empty-headed utterly meaninglessly? 222

[Sixth Judge]

 If you approve me, I
will go to Olympus to see
Apollo and persuade him to speak 225
 on the enigma of
Oedipus's fate, pleading humbly
for his wise help to us to make a fair judgment. 228

[Persephone to all judges]

   That is a prudent and
righteous idea. Would you all
approve of the proposal to persuade Apollo?   231

          [All Judges]

Yes, we agree on it.

     [Persephone to Sixth Judge]

Please go to Apollo and tell him
that it was the unanimous decision   234
   of our court to send you
to him for his wise advice on
how to resolve the perplexing weird case   237
   of Oedipus. Now, I adjourn
the present session of this court
until we hear from Apollo.

[Oedipus moved in tears]

Thank you,

 gracious Queen Persephone
and judges! Your wise and prudent
action is beyond what I could ever dream of.

240

243

{Sixth Judge leaves for Olympus with her attendants.
* The end of Scene #2.}*

Scene 3

Faked Oracles
Attributed to Apollo

A divine judge comes to verify with Apollo in Olympus the validity of Oedipus's claims about the bizarre and fateful oracle of his fate. Apollo asserts that he knows nothing of a paltry mortal, called Oedipus, let alone that he gave such an absurd oracle to anyone; he is indignant that vile humans make up such blatant fibs to blame gods as false excuses for their horrible crimes. He advises the judge to find out the truth, and then tell him who conjured up such a gruesome hoax.

Scene 3: *Faked Oracles Attributed to Apollo*

{Apollo in Olympus courteously receives
Sixth Judge from Hades.}

[Apollo]

Welcome to Olympus!
Do you bring an urgent message
to me from Queen Persephone?

[Sixth Judge]

                              Hail you,   246
   Apollo, the wise god
of prophecy! I was sent by
the court of the final judgment of the dead   249
   to entreat you to help
us on an intricate case beyond
our limited ken.

[Apollo]

                  The final judgment is   252
   entirely your power
to decide beyond my jurisdiction.

I wonder why your court has deemed that I   255
    may help you solve the case.

                [Sixth Judge]

Because it seems to implicate
your prophecy as the crucial factor.   258

                [Apollo]

    What? My prophecy? Tell
me more about the case.

                [Sixth Judge]

                        We have a bold
defendant, named Oedipus of Thebes; he   261
    killed his father, Laius,
the king of Thebes, and then married
his mother, Jocasta, the widowed queen.   264

Scene 3: *Faked Oracles Attributed to Apollo*

[Apollo]

What? I don't want to be
bothered to hear such vile, gruesome
misdeeds among accursed mortals. How did you   267
   dare to come to disturb me?

[Sixth Judge]

We are concerned with the crucial
matter of the divine justice; that is what   270
   brought me here to see you.

[Apollo]

Divine justice? What have I any thing
to do with that?

[Sixth Judge]

         It had something to do   273
  with your perplexing prophecy,
we surmised.

[Apollo]

What do you really mean?
How could my prophecy be implicated   276
   in such horrible crimes,
committed by evil mortals?

[Sixth Judge]

The defendant confessed that he did carry   279
   out such horrible misdeeds.
But he insisted that all his misdeeds
were mere accidents that ensued from his   282
   resolute actions to
avoid the fulfillment of your
awful prophecies about his fate, cursed on   285
   him even before he
was conceived in the womb of his
mother, Jocasta, by Laius.

[Apollo, chuckling]

What an absurd farce do you play on me,   288
   witty Judge from dark Hades!
I know nothing of such a vile
villain, you call Oedipus. How could he   291
   dare to lie that he heard
from me such an absurd gruesome
prophecy? I wonder how he could have   294
   been so successful in
deceiving you, wise judges of his
final judgment. Do you deem Oedipus   297
   as a *'super god'* who
claims to know his fate, even
before he was conceived in his mother's womb?   300

[Sixth Judge]

O wise Apollo! Your
cogent clarification opens
my blind eyes. Indeed, we needed your crucial   303
   help to solve the problem.
Oedipus shall learn soon what dire
punishments he will suffer for his grave   306

false accusation of
your prophecies about his ghastly
horrible misdeeds.

[Apollo]

        The cunning mortals   309
  make up such blatant fibs
to blame the gods for false excuses
of their horrible misdeeds. When you find   312
  out concrete facts about
your bizarre case, please come back,
and let me know how the sly mortals had   315
  conjured up such gruesome
tragedies to indulge themselves
in tormenting each other.

[Sixth Judge]

        Yes, I shall   318

report to you concrete facts
when we will find out about this grave
matter as it touches on the very validity
   of the divine justice.
Farewell, thank you for your wisdom!

321

{Sixth Judge leaves Olympus for Hade.
   The end of Scene #3. }

Scene 4

Oedipus's Suspicion of Acastus's Plot

Oedipus is deeply relieved to learn that Apollo had never condemned him with the awful prophecy. Hence, he suspects that it might have been a hoax, plotted by Acastus, a wily ambitious noble of Corinth. Oedipus was brought up as the beloved son of King Polybus and Queen Merope of Corinth. In his happy youth, Oedipus fell in love with Arete, the daughter of Acastus; he slandered that Oedipus was a base foundling who would bring harm and shame, and thus must be banished lest he should become a terrible tyrant of Corinth. Polybus threatened to exile Acastus and his family. But Acastus appealed to hear the Delphic judgement on the case. Acastus lured proud and anxious Oedipus to the Delphic shrine. A priest cursed Oedipus that he had been condemned to kill his father and mate with his mother. In shock and terror, Oedipus fled, vowing that he should never see Polybus and Merope again in his life lest the curse might be fulfilled.

{Sixth Judge returns. The court resumes its session.}

[Sixth Judge]

You cunning vile villain, Oedipus! How   324
   did you dare to conjure
up such a false accusation
of Apollo for the absurd prophecies   327
   about your gruesome abhorred
misdeeds that you committed at your will?

[Oedipus in great surprise]

I cannot understand what you mean, judge: 330
   Did Apollo deny
that he had made such prophecies
about Oedipus through his priest at the sacred   333
   shrine in Delphi?

[Sixth Judge]

          Apollo
asserted that he knew nothing of
a mortal, called Oedipus, let alone spoke   336

such false, absurd, gruesome
prophecies to anyone.

[Oedipus elated in ecstasy]

O, righteous
Apollo, you are the saviour of my soul!   339
Then, it was not your will
nor Zeus's to condemn Oedipus!
Nothing more could I have ever hoped to   342
find out, bearing all throes
of dire agonies throughout my harsh
tormenting life, at last!

[Persephone]

Why do you rejoice,   345
Oedipus, to hear such
stern denial by Apollo?
No more can you blame the god for your horrid   348
crimes that you committed
resolutely with your sane mind.

[Oedipus]

Please help me find out the mortal felons   351
   who schemed such a deadly
doom to Oedipus. It was the priest
at Delphi, not Apollo himself—no man   354
   alive can see a god speaking
to him—that told me the awful
oracle. Hold! It might be a dark plot   357
   of cunning Acastus
to expel me from Corinth in shame.

[Second Judge]

Who is this Acastus of Corinth? Why   360
   do you implicate him
for your misfortune?

[Oedipus]

            I wish to
tell you the story of my youth in Corinth: 363

How I was compelled to
consult with the oracle at
Delphi to ask who my real parents were.   366

[Persephone]

Yes. We want to know all
crucial concrete events that occurred
in your tumultuous life.

[Oedipus]

                    During my blessed   369
    happy youth in Corinth,
I grew up as a beloved proud
son of King Polybus and Queen Merope.   372
    They brought me up with great
loving cares of devoted parents:
I received the best education and I   375
    excelled all noble youths
of Corinth in intelligence,
prowess, and courage. The people adored me   378
    as their beloved bright prince.

In my twenty, I fell deeply
in love with Arete, a lovely tender   381
  maiden of a noble
family in Corinth. One day,
she told me in anguish that her father,   384
  Acastus, forbade our love;
He insisted that I was not a real
son of King Polybus but a base foundling   387
  who would bring harm and shame
to Corinth. Deeply offended, I
complained my parents about the terrible   390
  insult by Acastus.
In wrath, King Polybus threatened
to exile Acastus, accusing him   393
  for plotting to remove
his heir to the throne. But Acastus
appealed to the Corinthians that his claim   396
  be judged by an oracle
to be given by Apollo
at Delphi. If the oracle affirmed   399
  that I was a true son
of Polybus, then Acastus would
grant me to wed his daughter, Arete.   402

But if I turn out to be
a foundling as he insisted,
then I should be banished lest I become   405
  a terrible tyrant
of Corinth.

[Second Judge]

Vaguely, I recall
that Acastus of Corinth came here some   408
  years ago. How did Polybus
meet the challenge by Acastus?
Did he go to Delphi to consult with   411
  the oracle?

[Oedipus]

No. He
dismissed it as a cunning plot
and refused to consult with the oracle.   414
  But the ill rumours rampaged
wildly like the dreadful plague of
death to me; I became deeply suspicious   417

about myself that I must be
the real foundling, accursed to bring harm
and shame to Corinth. When I met the son   420
  of Acastus on the street,
he insulted me as a coward
who evaded their fair challenge to find out   423
  the truth of my parentage.
I swore him that I was determined
to go with him to hear the verdict of   426
  the oracle at Delphi,
defying the forbiddance by
Polybus. In secret, I left for Delphi   429
  with my three trusty servants.
When we reached the precinct of the shrine
after a long hard journey, the son of Acastus   432
  with his retinue of
many servants greeted us. It was
a pleasant surprise to see my beloved   435
  Arete, smiling in hope
and trembling in fear among them.
She wanted to hear the crucial verdict herself   438
  with me.

[Third Judge]

From whom did you
hear the prophecy of Apollo?

[Oedipus]

A priest in splendid robes met us outside   441
   the sacred shrine. He asked
in a solemn voice what we wanted to
learn from him. I said that I wished to know   444
   who my parents were in truth.
Suddenly, the priest beat me harshly,
shouting in indignant fury: *"Go away,*   447
   you accursed rogue! How do
you dare to pollute this holy shrine!
You are doomed to kill your father, and mate   450
   with your mother on his bed!"
In shocks of horrors and agonies,
I fell and swooned. When I regained my sense   453
   I saw my trusty servants
trembling in awe and pity.
"I banish my hateful damned self," said I,   456

"never to return to
my sweet homeland Corinth while King
Polybus or Queen Merope lives, lest I   459
might fulfill the awful
prophecy of my accursed fate."
I got up and ran away like a mad dog,   462
   struggling to flee from
the deadly grips of my doomed fate.

       [Third Judge]

Your piteous story of the weird events   465
   at Delphi sounds to me
like a sly hoax in a comedy.
Have you ever suspected that the priest might   468
   have been suborned by wily
Acastus? He could be a sham,
disguised in the garb of a priest.

       [Oedipus]

               No, never   471

occurred such a suspicion
in my mind until I learnt from
this court that Apollo had never condemned   474
  Oedipus!

[Persephone to all Judges]

     I propose
that we summon Acastus of
Corinth to testify on this crucial matter.   477

[All Judges]

Yes, we must.

[Second Judge]

     I will go
to find Acastus in our vast
realm of the dead and bring him to testify   480
  what he knew and did about
the fate of Oedipus.

{Second Judge leaves with his attendants.
  The end of Scene #4.}

Scene 5

Acastus's Confession of his Hoax

Acastus's ghost is summoned to testify at the Court. Apollo comes from Olympus to Hades to witness the trial of Oedipus. Acastus confesses that he played a subtle farce to save himself from political troubles with King Polybus; Acastus disguised himself as a priest at Delphi and proclaimed to Oedipus that he had been doomed to kill his father and mate with his own mother on his father's bed. When Oedipus heard such an awful hoax, he was shocked in panic dismay and fled from Corinth as a self-exile.

Scene 5: *Acastus's Confession of his Hoax*

{Second Judge enters the court with Acastus.
Oedipus is absent from the court.}

[*Persephone* to *Acastus*]

Who were you,
and what did you do while you lived on earth?   483

[*Acastus*]

My name is Acastus:
I was the king of Corinth that
is now ruled by my son, Abas.

[*Persephone*]

Did you   486

inherit the throne from
your father?

[Acastus]

No. When the previous
king, Polybus, died without leaving any heir,   489

the Corinthians acclaimed
me to be their new king.

[Sixth Judge]

Had Polybus
never have a son to succeed his throne?   492

[Acastus]

Yes, once he had an adopted
son, called Oedipus.

[Fifth Judge]

What did happen
to his adopted son?

[Acastus]

He was banished for life.   495

[Fourth Judge]

Did Polybus banish
Oedipus, his sole heir?

[Acastus]

Yes, he did.

[Third Judge]

Why did Polybus decide to do such   498
  an unusual thing? Was he
compelled to do it, or freely?

[Acastus]

He was compelled by an oracle of   501
  Apollo.

[Second Judge]

Was the oracle
kept in secret by Polybus,
or was it disclosed openly to the public?   504

Scene 5: *Acastus's Confession of his Hoax*

[Acastus]

All Corinthians leant it.

[First Judge]

Then tell us what the oracle said.

[Acastus]

It presaged that Oedipus should kill his   507
   father, and mate with his
mother on his father's bed.

[Persephone]

          Who did
utter such ghastly awful prophecies?   510

[Acastus]

  It was the Delphic priest
of Apollo.

Scene 5: *Acastus's Confession of his Hoax*

{Suddenly lightning and thunders peal, then Apollo
enters in disguise. Acastus swoons in shock.}

[Persephone]

Hail Apollo,
the god of divine prophecy! Welcome   513
   to our court. May we learn
what an urgent matter brought you
down here?

[Apollo]

Cordial greetings to you, wise Queen   516
   Persephone! I heard that
evil cunning mortals had forged
absurd prophecies as if they came from me,   519
   and slyly abused them
to terrify their ignorant
hapless victims. I request that you grant   522
   me to observe your trial
on the bizarre case of Oedipus.
As my prophecy was falsely implicated,   525

I volunteer to testify
at your court as a trusty witness.

[Persephone]

Thank you, Apollo, for your gracious aid.   528
  We shall find out the truth.

{Apollo sits next to the Sixth Judge.}

[Persephone to her attendants.]

Bring in the defendant.

{Blind Oedipus enters guided by the attendants.
Acastus recovers his sense and looks at Oedipus.}

[Persephone]

Do you
recognize who this man was, Acastus?   531

[Acastus]

No, I cannot make out
such a dreadfully disfigured man.

[Persephone to Oedipus]

Reveal yourself to Acastus of Corinth.   534

[Oedipus]

What? Is Acastus here?
Look at me, the ghastly husk of
Oedipus—once a proud prince of Corinth!   537
   But he was utterly
ruined by the dreadful oracle of
Apollo that your son, Abas, lured him   540
   to hear at Delphi.

[Acastus trembling in horror]

What?
Ah, Zeus! How much you have suffered,
wretched piteous Oedipus!

[Persephone]

                Now, tell us   543
the truth, Acastus. Did you
suborn the priest of Apollo
at Delphi to utter the sham, gruesome   546
   prophecies that Oedipus
had been condemned to kill
his father, and to mate with his mother?   549

[Acastus in hesitation]

  It was not meant to be
an oracle of Apollo,
but a subtle farce that I played, disguised   552
  as if I were a priest
at Delphi.

[Oedipus]

       What? Ah cunning cruel
Acastus, what a vile devil had you played   555
  on me with such a sly,
fatal hoax!

[*Persephone*]

Why did you conspire,
Acastus, the farce that brought to Oedipus   558
   such horrible tragedies?

[*Acastus*]

Young Oedipus was a clever,
astute, ambitious prince too proud of himself.   561
   When I learnt that he was
a mere foundling, not a real son
of King Polybus by his queen Merope,   564
   I tried to prevent him from
marrying my daughter, Arete.
Hence, I disclosed his secret parentage.   567
   King Polybus was so enraged
at me that he threatened to banish
my whole family. To defend myself   570
   I challenged him to consult
with the Delphic oracle to
reveal the true parentage of Oedipus.   573

[*Apollo* in disguise]

What did Polybus and you
hear at Delphi?

[*Acastus*]

          Polybus refused
to accept my challenge, proclaiming that   576
  we must not bother holy
gods with our inane paltry affairs.
But his fierce anger at me did not abate.   579
  I realized that I had
no other choice but vilify
Oedipus to save my family from   582
  the dire ire of Polybus.
For many dreadful days and sleepless
nights, I brooded over endless tracks of wandering 585
  thoughts. At last, the naïve plot
of the faked oracle dawned in my mind.
My son, Abas, succeeded in provoking   588
  proud and anxious Oedipus
to join with him to hear my hoax
oracle at the Delphic shrine.

Scene 5: *Acastus's Confession of his Hoax*

[*Apollo in disguise*]

                                    I wonder   591
    how your hoax have worked
so well.
                [Acastus]

        Somehow, it worked very
effectively beyond what I dreamt of—   594
    indeed, too well as I
regretted very much, later; first, it made
Oedipus flee from Corinth as a self-exile;   597
    Second, both Polybus
and Merope were genuinely
thankful to me that the presumed oracle   600
    saved his life and her virtue.
They admitted that Oedipus was
a foundling and he might bring grave harm and   603
    shame to them as I foresaw.
They proclaimed a life-long exile
for Oedipus; they also banished the shepherd   606
    who had brought them the cursed
foundling. All Corinthians respected
me as the wise courageous man who could   609

foresee the unseen to guard
their state.

[Oedipus]

Now I see that, o gods,
it was not your doing, but my dire fate 612
  has been contrived by men,
including myself—so stupid,
credulous, and blinded in my fatal pride! 615
  All have come to light, too true
for me to see them. I have been
a wild child of chance, a fleeting brother 618
  of the changing moon; I
wax, and I wane with it. I do not
blame you, sly Acastus; you were far more 621
  superior than I was
in plotting cunningly to trap
one's foes. Now, tell me one more thing: how is 624
  Arete whom I love?

[Acastus]

Forgive me, Oedipus! I repent
my horrible misdeeds inflicted on you.   627
  I feel your pangs of pains
and throes of dire agonies. Soon after
you were banished from Corinth, my distraught   630
  daughter in utter despairs
suddenly disappeared from us,
never to be found alive or dead—the dire   633
  terrible retribution
of my wily plot to my family.
Soon my wretched wife died of grief. I lost all   636
  my joy and verve of living.

[Persephone]

What intriguing tragic comedies
you cunning mortals have played out to each   639
  other in the magic names
of your bogus gods! Didn't you claim,
Oedipus, that you had been somehow doomed   642
  to kill your father
even before you were conceived
in your mother's womb?

[Oedipus]

Yes, I did.

[Persephone]

How do you know   645
that it would not turn out to be
another hoax made up by a wily
felon far worse than Acastus here?

[Oedipus]

I learnt   648
it from Jocasta, then
my Queen. But it is impossible
for me to know whether her saying is   651
true or not, although I
have believed in it.

[Fourth Judge]

Tell us what
Jocasta said to you.

[Oedipus]

An oracle came 654
to Laius—she would not say
from the god Apollo himself
but from his ministers at Delphi: it 657
  proclaimed that it would be
the fate of Laius to be killed
by his son to be born of Jocasta. 660
  In fear of such an awful
oracle, when their son was born,
Laius fastened ankles of the three-day 663
  old babe and had him cast
out by his thrall to let him die
in the wilderness of Mount Cithaeron. 666

[Third Judge]

Was it you, Oedipus,
who suffered such a cruel crime—
the very victim of Laius's infanticide? 669

[Oedipus]

Yes. I was that very infant.

[Second Judge]

If so, how did you survive it?

[Oedipus]

Out of pity, the thrall of King Laius   672
  saved the infant in bold
disobedience to his master.
How I wish that I had perished before   675
  he gave me to the shepherd
from Corinth rather than to become
a foundling-prince of King Polybus, and   678
  then a killer of his real
father unknown to me!

[Persephone to all judges]

             We must
summon Laius to testify here, right now.   681

Scene 5: *Acastus's Confession of his Hoax*

[All judges]

Yes, we must interrogate
Laius about this gruesome matter.

[Apollo in disguise]

I also want to hear what Laius would dare   684
    to claim about the absurd
inane fib of the faked prophecy, alleged
to Apollo.

[Third Judge]

        I will go to capture Laius   687
    of Thebes and bring him here.
I know quite well who he was and
what he had done while he was alive in Thebes.   690

*{Third Judge leaves the court with his attendants.
The court adjourns. The end of Scene #5. }*

Scene 6

Laius's Confession of his Infanticide

Laius's ghost is summoned. He encounters the disfigured Oedipus and recognizes him as the youth who killed him at Phocis on his way to Delphi, but he denies resolutely that Oedipus was his infant son who had survived somehow his attempt of cruel infanticide.

*{Laius is led in by Third Judge. The court resumes
       in the absence of Oedipus.}*

[Persephone *to Laius*]

Speak to us who you were,
and what you had done while you lived
on the green earth.

[Laius]

                  I am Laius, once a king   693
  of the seven gated mighty Thebes.
I was the son of Labdacus,
the son of Polydore, the son of Cademus,   696
  and the son of Agenor.

[Persephone]

I see. Then what was the name of
your son?

[Laius]

I had no son.

[Persephone]

               Did your queen   699
Jocasta bear a son
by you, or not?

[Laius]

Once she bore a son
but he died in his infancy.

[Persephone to the attendants]

                Bring in   702
the defendant and witness.

{Acastus leads Oedipus in.}

Scene 6: *Laius's Confession of his Infanticide*

[*Persephone*]

Laius, do you recognize this man?

[*Laius*]

By Zeus, I do not know who this poor   705
   ghastly looking ghost was.

[*Persephone*]

Do you insist, Oedipus, that
you are the very son of King Laius and   708
   Queen Jocasta of Thebes?

[*Oedipus*]

Yes, I do.

{*Oedipus kneels in front of Laius as a suppliant.*}

      O great King Laius,
my real father unknown to me.   Forgive   711

me for my terrible
misdeed, unwittingly inflicted
upon you at the fatal spot in Phocis.   714

[*Laius*]

What? Are you that young rascal
who slew me on my way to Delphi?

[*Oedipus*]

Yes, I was that very rash insolent youth.   717

[*Laius*]

How do you dare to insult
me by your shameless bold mocking
that you were my son?

[*Oedipus*]

                    If you wish, I will   720
prove it.

Scene 6: *Laius's Confession of his Infanticide*

[*Laius*]

Stop prattling
such inane nonsense!

[*Oedipus*]

Did you ever
have a son by your queen Jocasta?   723

[*Laius*]

Why do you ask it? No—
except an infant who lived for
only three days.

[*Oedipus*]

How did the infant die?   726

[*Laius*]

Why do you keep on asking
questions on such private matters?

[Oedipus]

To prove that I was the very child you cast 729
  away to die.

[Laius]

      No! It cannot
be! Utterly impossible!

[Oedipus]

Did you not give away your son to your thrall 732
  to be thrown in the wild
of Mount Cithaeron—its both ankles
pierced and pinned together to be an easy 735
  prey for wild beasts—if it
had not already died of cold and
starvation?

[Laius]

    Ah Zeus! How did you survive 738

your cursed doom? How did you
learn my awful misdeed, Oedipus?

[Persephone]

We need concrete witnesses to testify   741
   for this intriguing case.
Laius, go and find your thrall who
took the babe from you but rescued him   744
   from your terrible plot
of infanticide.

[Third Judge]

     We must find
the thrall and bring him here to assist us   747
   in bringing forth light to
these gruesome matters.

{Third Judge leaves with Laius and his attendants.
 The end of Scene #6.}

Scene 7

Testimony by Laius's Thrall

The ghost of the thrall of Laius is summoned. He admits that King Laius gave him an infant and bade him discard it in the wilderness of Mount Cithaeron. But his conscience compelled him to disobey such a cruel command. Hence, the thrall gave the infant to a fellow shepherd from Corinth. King Polybus took the child from his shepherd and reared him as his son. Laius confesses that he attempted the cruel infanticide because he was so afraid of the awful curse of Pelops that his son to be born would kill him.

{Third Judge returns to the court with Laius and his thrall.}

[Persephone]

Is this your thrall
who saved Oedipus from your premeditated   750
  infanticide, Laius?

[Laius]

Yes, he was our trusted thrall, not bought
but bred in our household.

[Persephone to the thrall]

Why did you disobey   753
your master's stern behest?

[Thrall]

I obeyed my conscience, crying
out pity for the helplessly crying baby.   756

I could not leave him crying
in the harsh wilderness of Mount
Cithaeron.

[Laius]

Then what did you do with him? 759

[Thrall]

I gave him to a shepherd
from Corinth, begging him to rear
the child as his foster son for god's sake. 762

[Acastus]

I know the shepherd of King
Polybus; he claimed that he saved
the infant from death in Mount Cithaeron, 765
   freeing the pins that riveted
his feet and thus named him *"Oedipus."*
Polybus and Merope took the child from 768

their shepherd and reared him
as if he were their genuine offspring.
Reveal your ankles, Oedipus, for everyone   771
    to see what I have said.

{Oedipus reveals the old scars of his pierced ankles.}

[Oedipus]

Look at these scars, my sire Laius,
of my riveted ankles—sad proof that I was   774
    the very child so condemned!

[Laius]

Ah me! It was Zeus who brought
such cursed fates upon us. Now I see how   777
    you had survived my vile,
cowardly misdeed, and grew up
to slay me as foretold by the dreadful   780
    prophecy. And yet how
happy I am that the gods saved
my only son from my horrid cruelty.   783

My dear son, Oedipus,
forgive me, your selfish base father.
Allow me to embrace you in heartfelt love.   786

{Laius and Oedipus embrace each other.}

[Persephone]

Why did you intend to
kill your innocent and helpless
infant son, Laius? How do you dare to   789
    blame Zeus for your cruel
infanticide?

[Laius]

        An oracle
forewarned me that my son to be born would   792
    kill me someday, if he
was allowed to grow up.

[Apollo in disguise]

What? How
did you obtain such an absurd oracle?   795
  Do you claim that you heard
it from Apollo himself or his priests?

[Laius]

No. The dire curse of Pelops threatened me   798
  in my dreadful dreams for
countless nights.

[Apollo in disguise]

If so, then it was
merely your own nightmares, not a divine   801
  oracle, at all.

[Laius]

No,
it did not come from Apollo.

[Oedipus to Laius]

But I heard from Jocasta that the awful   804
  oracle came to you
from the ministers of Apollo
at Delphi. Did she know that it was just   807
  what you had imagined in
your dreams?

[Laius]

Out of necessity,
I misled Jocasta to yield her baby   810
  for a quick sacrifice
lest my awful doom is fulfilled.

[Acastus]

By Zeus, your dream of hoax-oracle,   813
  King Laius, surpassed by far
my plain play of farce-oracle!

[Persephone]

Confess, Laius, the true causes of your fierce   816
  lunatic fear of your
own son!

[Laius]

It was the dreadful curse
of Pelops upon me due to the mis-   819
   construed abduction of
his beloved son, Chrysippus, by me.

[Persephone]

Confess all what you did to Chrysippus: 822
   Why Pelops cursed you; and
why you feared it so much.

[Laius]

                    Since my sire
died when I was young, Lycus raised me as   825
   my regent. Just before
Amphion and Zethus attacked Thebes,
killed Lycus, and usurped the throne, I was   828
   entrusted to king Pelops
of Elis in Peloponnesus
as my trusty protector. For several years   831

I grew up in his great
palace as a welcomed guest: he
taught me important skills, best of all, how   834
   to drive fast war-chariots.
As I became an expert, he
  entrusted his young son, Chrysippus, to learn   837
   charioting and other
sports under my guidance for five years.
One day, I led Chrysippus to compete   840
   at the famed Nemean games.
He won the top championship.
While we celebrated the victory, a herald   843
   from Thebes came to me; he
 informed that I had been proclaimed
as their rightful new king since both Amphion   846
   and Zethus perished. I
returned to Thebes immediately,
taking Chrysippus with me. King Pelops   849
   sent me his herald that
Chrysippus should come back to him
right away; but I wanted him to stay with me   852
   in Thebes as I had been
deeply attached to him; I offered
Chrysippus to share the throne of Thebes as   855

my co-ruler. Pelops
misconstrued my brotherly love
of Chrysippus as immoral abduction: 858
  He dispatched his strong troops,
commanded by his two sons, Atreus
and Thyestes, to attack me to surrender   861
  Chrysippus. But I was
resolutely determined to
ignore such a threat and to defend Thebes.   864
  For days and nights, I worked
hard to fortify our ramparts,
posting our brave, loyal soldiers to guard   867
  the adamant seven gates.
When our preparation for war
was completed, a guard rushed to report that   870
  Chrysippus had driven
out his chariot to join with his
half-brothers. I climbed up our watch-tower   873
  and saw the troops sent by
Pelops retreating afar; I bade
heartfelt farewell to Chrysippus with best wishes. 876
  Soon I married Jocasta,
the graceful daughter of noble
Menoeceus, blooming in her beautiful youth.   879

[Persephone]

If Chrysippus returned
safely to Pelops, why did he
spell the curse on you and why did you fear it?   882

[Laius]

Shortly after Chrysippus
left Thebes, he appeared in my dream
as a sad ghost lamenting his terrible   885
   murder. The next morning
a herald from Pelops came to me;
He proclaimed that Chrysippus had killed himself. 888
   Much worse, Pelops accused
me for his death. According to
Atreus and Thyestes, they interrogated   891
   Chrysippus why he had not
returned to Elis immediately
after his victory at the Nemean games;   894
   Chrysippus replied that
Laius had abducted him to Thebes,
and abused him as his lover; then, in shame,   897
   Chrysippus killed himself.

They brought back his corpse to Pelops
for a solemn funeral in Elis.   900
   Pelops invoked Zeus
to punish me for the alleged
crime. In shock, sorrow, and fear, I swooned.   903
   One day, a trusty servant
of my queen Jocasta told me
that she happened to see how Chrysippus   906
   was actually murdered
by Atreus and Thyestes in
the thick forest not far from our rampart.   909
   Creon, the wise brother
of my queen, advised me that I
should go to Delphi and plead Apollo   912
   to reveal the true cause
of Chrysippus's death to Pelops
so that he would revoke his curse upon me.   915

[Apollo in disguise]

   Did you see Apollo?
If so, what did he say to you?

[Laius]

Not Apollo himself—how could a man   918
   really see the god—but
I met with his holy priestess
at the Delphic shrine. I asked her whether   921
   I should go, or not, to see
King Pelops and try to persuade
him that Chrysippus was murdered by his   924
   half-brothers, Atreus
and Thyestes. The priestess
sternly rebuked me that my accusation   927
   against the famed sons of Pelops
was incredible because I had not
witnessed it myself, at all; servants tended   930
   to make up absurd fibs
to relieve their masters from distress.
Most of all, my blame of his sons would   933
   enrage Pelops to punish
me with an immediate death.
Then I asked the prudent priestess whether   936
   she would appeal for me
to Apollo to reveal the truth
to Pelops as a divine oracle.   939

Sternly, she scolded me that
I was a witless vile rascal;
While I had failed in convincing her, I   942
  still tried to bribe her to
make such an absurd appeal
to Apollo. She heard that Pelops had   945
  invoked Zeus to fulfill
his curse that Laius should be killed
by his son, yet to be born. Her best advice   948
  for me, she said, was not
to beget any son. Since that time,
the awful curse of Pelops resounded in me   951
  as if it were the very curse
of Zeus, tormenting my heart.

[Persephone]

Do you insist that Pelops spelled wrong curse   954
  upon you, Laius, and thus
that your attempted infanticide
of your son should be deemed as just?   957

[Laius]

No! I was so selfish,
cowardly, and stupid. Punish me
for my horrible crime. The only thing I   960
  would like to plead you is
that my son is truly innocent
of patricide: never did he intended it   963
  nor was he aware of who
I was to him in dark accidents
of our tumultuous life. He was a hapless   966
  victim of my cursed fate.
I beseech you to absolve my son,
Oedipus, from all his unwitting sins.   969

[Persephone]

Do you know any witness
who saw how it actually
happened that Oedipus killed you?

[Thrall]

I saw it.   972

Scene 7: *Testimony by Laius's Thrall*

[Persephone]

Good! Tell us exactly
what you witnessed.

[Thrall]

          I followed King
Laius on his way to visit Delphi.   975
   When our retinue of five
men drew near the triple-branching roads
at Phocis, we met a young man distraught   978
   in anguishes. Our herald
and two strong attendants jostled
the young man from the narrow pass. In rage,   981
   he struck down all three with
his walking stick. When the youth passed
nearby, King Laius hit him from his car.   984
   But deftly, he flung Laius
out of the car and laid him dead
in one stroke. I fled from the deadly spot   987
   for my dear life in panic.

[Persephone]

Do you agree, Laius, with what
your thrall spoke?

[Laius]

    Yes, that was how the accident   990
  happened. I affirm that
the young man acted deftly in proper
self-defense: I paid my dues, deserving   993
  such an ignoble death.

[Persephone]

What did you plan to do in Delphi?

[Laius]

I wished to consult with the oracle,   996
  hoping to learn how to
beget my heir as we remained
childless since I had discarded our first baby.   999

[Sixth Judge]

Did you see any omen
in your dream, or did any seer warn
you of your impending calamity   1002
   on your way to Delphi?

[Laius]

No, not at all. Our famed seer,
Tiresias, strongly advised me to visit   1005
   the Delphic shrine with rich
gifts and implore Apollo for
his merciful help.

[First Judge]

          How did the people   1008
  of Thebes learn the death of
their king at such a remote place?

[Thrall]

I brought the terrible news back to Thebes.   1011

[Laius]

How did the Thebans pursue
to capture and punish the killer
of their king?

[Thrall]

        Nothing they tried to find out   1014
the killer at that time.

[Laius]

Nothing? No Thebans minded my death?
Where were Jocasta, Creon, and Tiresias?   1017

[Thrall]

I was a lowly thrall
who knew nothing about what went
with the vital secret affairs of the state.   1020

[Laius]

I entreat you, mighty goddess
Persephone, to summon Creon
and Tiresias to testify how they had   1023
  dealt with the murder
 of their king.

[First Judge]

      I object to the plea
as it may distract us from focusing   1026
  on Oedipus's trial.

[Fifth Judge to Oedipus]

When and how did you find out that
you were the very killer of King Laius?   1029

[Oedipus]

  Twelve years after I took up
the helm of our ship of state Thebes,
formidable pestilences struck our ship,   1032

forlorn helplessly, drenched in
weltering surges of blood. Dire blight ruined
our harvest, flocks, and herds; our women wailed   1035
   in travail of miscarriage.
All my subjects entreated me to
find apt remedy to cure them from deadly   1038
   diseases, not deeming me
as a new divinity but
the first of men in the common accidents   1041
   of our uncertain life.
Threading an endless maze of weary
thoughts in anguish and tears, I came upon   1044
   a clue of hope: to ask
Apollo how I might save Thebes
by act or word. On my behalf, Creon   1047
   consulted with the Delphic
oracle: it said that we must find
and punish the killer of Laius to save   1050
   Thebes from the deadly blight.
Sternly, I proclaimed that I should
be the blood-avenger of King Laius,   1053
   and condemned his unknown
killer with utmost relentless curses.
In spite of my stern behest, nobody came   1056

Scene 7: *Testimony by Laius's Thrall*

up with any clue how to
find the killer of Laius. As
Thebans suggested that their seer, Tiresias,   1059
   might help me discover
the concealed criminal, humbly I
beseeched him to reveal the accursed killer,   1062
   and save us from the dire
defilement of the blood-shed.

[Fourth Judge]

What did
Tiresias say to you, bold Oedipus?   1065

[Oedipus]

At first, he refused to speak
with me, lamenting *"Alas, what*
misery to be wise, when wisdom profits   1068
   nothing!" His obstinate
withholding of the crucial knowledge
despite of my earnest supplications   1071

to him enraged me; I charged
that he must be the schemer of
the plot to kill Laius, if not the assassin.   1074
   Then, in wrath, Tiresias
retaliated me: *"You are the very*
murderer of the man whose murderer   1077
  you are pursuing, now:
With your bright sight, you are blind to
your corrupted life: who your real parents are;   1080
  whom you live with. All
unknowing, you are the bane of
your own flesh and blood, the dead in the Hades   1083
  and the living on earth.
The double lash of your mother's and
your father's curses will thrash you, Oedipus,   1086
  from this land, tramping you
down in terror, utter darkness
shrouding your eyes that can see the light now.   1089
  Your baneful weird is not
to fall by me. I leave to Apollo,
what concerns the god!" Such horrible stern   1092
  indictment of me by
Tiresias terrified me like
a death blow.

[Third Judge]

You had been a fierce hunter   1095
  who pursued resolutely
to hunt down yourself as your own
victim. But who did prove your misdeed with   1098
  concrete evidences?

[Oedipus]

I did.

[Second Judge]

How could you do that, Oedipus?

[Oedipus]

In spite of Jocasta's stern objections   1101
  I summoned this thrall to
testify on the crucial matters:
He proved himself not only the sole witness   1104
  of Laius's death but also
the saviour of Laius's infant son,
handed to him to be discarded in the wild   1107

of Mount Cithaeron. Thus
I realized who I was in truth,
at last; and how the hoax-prophecies, made   1110
  up by the sly faked priest
of Apollo had been fulfilled,
all by my own wretched self!

       [Apollo in disguise]

                 How fascinating   1113
  to hear what you confess,
Oedipus! May I request that
Tiresias be summoned here to testify   1116
  how he could attribute
the hoax-prophecies of Acastus
to Apollo?

       [Persephone]

           Yes, I also think that   1119
  Tiresias should help us
unravel the intricate case
of Oedipus.

[All Judges]

We agree. Let us summon him.   1122

[Fifth Judge]

I know of the proud blind
seer, Tiresias; I will go
to find and bring him here to reveal   1125
   his mystic weird art
of bewildering divination.

*{Fifth Judge exits with his attendants.
The end of Scene # 7}*

Scene 8

Tiresias's Boast of his Divination

Tiresias's ghost is summoned. He brags that he was a wise seer who foresaw things to come and helped ignorant mortals to avoid misfortunes. Oedipus confutes Tiresias's false claim that he predicted crucial events before they occurred. His pretence of foreseeing was based on what he gathered from others who witnessed what had already happened.

Scene 8: *Tiresias's Boast of his Divination*

{The court resumes its session. Fifth Judge brings in Tiresias.}

[Persephone]

Tell us who you were and what you did while   1128
  you lived on earth.

[Tiresias]

                I am
Tiresias, the world-renown seer
of Thebes. I served Apollo in conveying   1131
  his divine prophecies
to the ignorant, helpless mortals.

[Persephone]

Do you remember what happened to Laius,   1134
  your king of Thebes and his
unknown son, Oedipus?

[Tiresias]

Yes, I do
remember their terrible tragedies!   1137

[Persephone]

Then you know that Oedipus
killed his father, Laius.

[Tiresias]

Of course!
I had foreseen the patricide long ahead   1140
   it actually occurred
at the fatal spot where three roads
met in Phocis.

[Apollo in disguise]

How could you foresee it?   1143

[Tiresias]

I have to refrain from
revealing the secret mystery
of the sacred art of divination. 1146

[Apollo in disguise]

Well, then tell us what you
foretold of the death of Laius:
Did you foresee the time and place in which 1149
Laius was doomed to die?

[Tiresias]

No. What I foresaw was who his
killer should be.

[Apollo in disguise]

You mean Oedipus.

[Tiresias]

Yes, 1152

his unknown son, discarded
by Laius to the wilderness
of Mount Cithaeron when he was an infant.   1155

[Persephone to attendants]

Bring in the defendant
and the witnesses.

{Laius enters guiding blind Oedipus by hand. Acastus follows.}

[Tiresias *to Laius*]

Ah Apollo,
what pitiful sights! Are you not King Laius?   1158
   But who is this ghastly
blind figure you look after with
such tender care?

[Laius]

Welcome, Tiresias!   1161
   Behold this is my son,
Oedipus. I am glad that you
have come to this court of the divine judgment   1164

to help exonerate him
from the unwitting patricide.

[Tiresias]

I serve only Apollo, not mortal men.   1167

[First Judge]

How did you find out that
Laius had been slain, Tiresias?

[Tiresias]

Creon told me that the king was murdered   1170
  by bandits at Phocis.

[Second Judge]

What did Creon or the elders
of Thebes do to find out the killer, arrest,   1173
  and punish the criminal?

[Tiresias]

They had no clue for any suspect.

[Third Judge]

But you, Tiresias, knew that Oedipus   1176
  must be the killer of
Laius as you have avowed.

[Tiresias]

                  Yes, I

knew it.

[Fourth Judge]

    Did you tell Creon or the elders   1179
  of Thebes that the killer
of their king must be the bold young
man, Oedipus, if your art of divination   1182
  was credible?

[Tiresias]

No. I
did not reveal it to anyone.

[Laius]

Why not, Tiresias? Did not Creon or   1185
    any elders of Thebes consult
with you about how they could capture
and punish the murderer of their king?   1188

[Tiresias]

No, they never asked me.
Soon after your death, the deadly
riddling Sphinx inflicted horrible havocs   1191
    on Thebes; the most urgent
crucial task for us then was how
to solve the lethal riddle, imposed by   1194
    the sly enchanting monster.

[Laius]

How long did it take you to solve
the riddle?

[Tiresias]

     While I was struggling to   1197
  divine the right answer,
a young stranger wandered into
Thebes and solved the riddle ahead of me.   1200

[Laius]

Who was that wise young stranger?

[Tiresias]

It was Oedipus, your killer!
He was hailed as the saviour of their state   1203
  by all Thebans; they acclaimed
Oedipus to succeed your throne,
King Laius.

[Fifth Judge]

At that time, Tiresias, you   1206
   must have already known that
the bold young stranger, acclaimed as
your new king, was the son and killer of   1209
Laius?

[*Tiresias*]

Yes, I knew it.

[*Sixth Judge*]

Did the widowed queen, Jocasta,
or any other citizens of Thebes consult   1212
   with you, Tiresias,
about the merit of her second
marriage to the unknown hero, acclaimed   1215
   as the new king of Thebes?

[*Tiresias*]

No. I heard about it after they
got married so quickly.

[Laius]

What? Jocasta   1218
married our own son? Ah gods,
forbid such an abhorred vile sin!

{In shock, Laius swoons.}

[Acastus]

Ah, awful hands of fates! In fact, Oedipus   1221
   mated with his real mother,
as if he had to fulfill my hoax
prophecy! I devised it merely to make   1224
   Queen Merope afraid of
her overly adored foundling son:
the handsome, clever, and proud Oedipus.   1227

[Persephone]

How did it happen, Oedipus,
that you married Queen Jocasta?

[Oedipus]

The accursed sinful marriage came with   1230
   the throne of Thebes to me:
Creon proclaimed to me that it was
their proper custom for a new foreign   1233
   bachelor successor
to the throne to wed the widowed queen
as co-rulers of Thebes. Such sudden drastic   1236
   changes in my fortune from
Apollo's awful condemnation
at Delphi to the sheer exultation   1239
   of the astonishing
acclamation as a new king
of the great Thebes overwhelmed me in wonder.   1242
   I realized that I was
the child of pure chance that had ruled
my life; I could not foresee a day ahead,   1245
   struggling at random
in the dark to face as best as
I could see every trial of life as it   1248
   happened. I gave up any
hope for help from the gods. I solved
the riddle of Sphinx with my own mental   1251

power without a help
of their vague mystic prophecies.
And I kept on striving to do all my best   1254
  to meet with whatever
came by chance in my hard, harsh life.
Since I took the solemn responsibility   1257
  in steering our ship of state,
the glorious Thebes, as the first
of men and also the first in the common   1260
  accidents of life, I
have wept through countless sleepless nights,
and struggled to thread intricate, complex mazes   1263
  of inquisitive thoughts
how to map out the right course for Thebes.
The gracious devotion and love of Queen   1266
  Jocasta to me with
her wise prudence and encouragement
nurtured and uplifted me to carry out   1269
  my task with confidence.

[Fourth Judge]

Before you decided to marry
Queen Jocasta, had you seen any sign of   1272

uneasy premonition?
You knew that she was much older
than you were about the age of your mother.   1275

[Oedipus]

No premonition, at all!
Queen Jocasta looked much younger
and graceful than Queen Merope who, I   1278
  believed, was my real mother.
It was impossible for me to
suspect that Jocasta could be my mother;   1281
  Even now, it seems to me
a false, misleading, and terrible
nightmare, conjured up by my sick brain!   1284

[Sixth Judge]

Did you beget any child?

[Oedipus]

Yes. We had two brave sons and two
lovely devoted daughters.

[Fourth Judge]

What? Did Jocasta   1287
  give birth to four children
after she married you?

[Oedipus]

Yes, she was
their mother.

[Fourth Judge]

How strange it seems! She had been   1290
  barren for more than twenty
years with Laius. But somehow, she
became so fertile after she mated with   1293
  her own son? I have many
questions to ask this mysterious
woman, Jocasta.   If you all agree that   1296
  we should summon her here,
 I will go to find Queen Jocasta,
and bring her here to unravel her dark   1299
  womanly mysteries.

[Persephone]

It is, indeed, very strange. We must
summon her to testify to us what she   1302
   knew and did about Oedipus.

[All Judges]

Yes, we all agree absolutely.
She may reveal to us crucial secrets.   1305

*{Fourth Judge exits with her attendants.
   The end of Scene #8.}*

Scene 9

Jocasta's Testimony

Jocasta's ghost is summoned. She reveals her stunning secrets: the birth-father of Oedipus is not Laius but Chrysippus, the son of Pelops. She fell deeply in love with the handsome Chrysippus while he was detained by Laius in Thebes after winning the chariot race at the Nemean Games. When King Pelops sent his army, led by Atreus and Thyestes, Chrysippus's two half-brothers, she attempted to elope with Chrysippus, waiting for him in the woods. When Chrysippus came to the hiding place, Atreus and Thyestes murdered Chrysippus and pretended that he had committed suicide for shameful affairs with Laius. Enraged Pelops vented an awful curse on Laius that he was doomed to be killed by his own son.

Scene 9: *Jocasta's Testimony*

{The court resumes its session. Jocasta is led in by Fourth Judge.}

[Persephone]

Who were you and what did
you do, while you lived on earth?

[Jocasta]

My name is Jocasta. I was a queen
  of Thebes.

1308

[Persephone]

Who were your consorts?

[Jocasta]

King Laius was my first husband.
After his accidental death, I was wedded

1311

to his successor, King
Oedipus.

[Persephone]

Was he not the son
of Laius?

[Jocasta]

I confess that Oedipus   1314
was my own son to whom
it happened that I was married
unwittingly as a favour of our state   1317
to the unknown hero
who had saved Thebes from the calamity.

[Persephone to attendants]

Bring in the defendant and all witnesses.   1320

*{Laius enters, leading blind Oedipus by hand.
Acastus, Tiresias, and the thrall of Laius follow.
Laius recognizes Jocasta.}*

[Laius]

Jocasta, my dear Queen,
Behold our long-lost son; gods saved
him from the wilderness of Mount Cithaeron!   1323

[Jocasta]

Ah, what a heartbreaking
piteous sight—my beloved son, ·
Oedipus, what terrible woes you have   1326
    suffered in the throes of agony!
My Lord, Laius, pity on me,
your hapless wife and his accursed mother   1329
    of shame and dire anguish.

{Jocasta embraces Oedipus and Laius.}

[Oedipus]

O my dear gracious mother, how
good to hear your gentle, tender voice again: 1332

You always comfort me
to overcome bitter acute pangs
of our horrible miseries and dire throes   1335
   of our terrible agonies.

[Persephone]

Jocasta, have you ever heard
any prophecy or seen a sign that warned   1338
   you of your incestuous
second marriage?

[Jocasta]

   No, not at all!
I have neither consulted for an oracle   1341
   nor trusted the dubious
art of divination in my life.

[Tiresias]

Ah bold woman, Jocasta! Your audacious   1344
   blasphemy was the very cause
of your undoing in vile shame.

Scene 9: *Jocasta's Testimony*

[Jocasta]

What did you dare to say, Tiresias? Now,   1347
  confess the truth to us:
Did you know, or not, the brave wise
stranger who had solved the riddle of Sphinx   1350
  and had saved Thebes from her
lethal pestilence, and hence he
was acclaimed as our new king, Oedipus—   1353
  that he was the very man
who had undone Laius at Phocis
in their inadvertent brawl?

[Tiresias]

               I will not speak: 1356
  I serve only Apollo, not
woman, nor man.

[Thrall]

           May a thrall speak
on this matter?

[Persephone]

      Certainly, if you speak   1359
the truth.

[Thrall]

    When I saw the new
young king, I recognized that he
was the very man who had killed our old king,   1362
  Laius, at Phocis about two
months ago.

[Laius]

     Did you report to Creon
or other Thebans about the crucial fact?   1365

[Thrall]

  No. In fear and anguish,
I confessed it to our seer
in a private meeting.

Scene 9: *Jocasta's Testimony*

[First Judge]

What did the seer   1368
say to you after he
had heard such a shocking grave news?

[Thrall]

He told me that those things came out exactly   1371
   as he had already foreseen
in his divination; sternly, he
warned me not to tell anyone about it   1374
   as the Thebans would stone
me to death in anger if they heard
what I claimed to be true. Hence, I begged   1377
   Queen Jocasta to send me
to a remote field far from the sight
of our new king.

[Second Judge]

Who was that sly seer?   1380

[Thrall]

Tiresias, right here, was
that seer!

[Persephone]

What? Tiresias,
do you deny what he has said?

[Tiresias]

                  No. This thrall   1383
was the sole surviving
witness of Laius's death.

[Laius]

              Ah, wily
traitor, Tiresias, you evil, vile villain!   1386
  Why did you conceal such
a grave crucial matter, betraying
the safety of our State? How highly had   1389

we honoured you as our
divine seer who knew the secrets
of the heaven and earth hidden to us?   1392

[Tiresias]

May peace be with you, King
Laius! Do you know how terrible
knowledge is when it brings no profit but   1395
   harm to the man who knows it?

[Laius]

You, sly shameless villain! You have
sold sham prophecies for your greedy profits,   1398
   cheating credulous foolish
people as if you were a trusty
prophet of Apollo!

[Jocasta]

         My dear lord, Laius,   1401

how earnestly did I
implore you not to trust cunning
seers and their glib dubious prophecies!   1404
    What dreadful tragedies
we have suffered by them; you wanted
to kill the innocent, helpless infant son—   1407
    your only heir—in inane
fears of the absurd false oracle
that threatened you, rejecting earnest pleas   1410
    of his heartbroken mother.
You drove an iron pin through the tender
ankles of the three-day-old helpless baby   1413
    and cast the child away to starve
in the wilds of Mount Cithaeron,
cheating yourself to be freed from such a cruel   1416
    infanticide. If you
had ignored such absurd prophecies
and had raised the child in our palace with   1419
    loving cares as King Polybus
of Corinth did as his beloved
foster son, Oedipus, you would not have   1422
    been killed in such pettish
squabbles at Phocis on your way

to hear more vain oracles at Delphi   1425
  so ingloriously.

[Laius]

Forgive me, Jocasta. I repent
my foolish follies and cowardly crimes.   1428

[Tiresias]

  No mortal can defy
divine prophecies; all of you
have witnessed that whatever I foretold   1431
  you to happen, all had
been fulfilled. I am a true prophet
of Apollo. What I foresee is true, and   1434
  in that lie my divine
missions and supernal power.

[Apollo in disguise]

What did you foretell as a prophet of   1437
  Apollo?

[Tiresias]

The murder
of Laius by his son and the vile,
shameful marriage of his widow to her son,   1440
   the killer of her husband!

[Oedipus]

To whom did you foretell that such
ghastly events would take place, Tiresias,   1443
   prior to I happened
to do such misdeeds utterly
unwittingly and inadvertently?   1446

[Tiresias]

Did I not tell you the truth
when you summoned me to reveal
the killer of Laius at the assembly   1449
   of Theban citizens?

Scene 9: *Jocasta's Testimony*

[Oedipus]

You boasted that you had foretold
certain events to someone before they   1452
  actually took place.
But you did not foretell me, at all,
that I would kill my father in the future.   1455
  Have you ever foretold
your king, Laius, that his son will
kill him in the future, or foretold your queen,   1458
  Jocasta, that her son
will marry his mother someday?

[Tiresias]

No, I did not. Such dark matters irked me.   1461

[Jocasta]

  What? Ah, you monstrous, vile,
and, sly fiend! Why did you conceal
that the strange hero who had solved the riddle   1464
  of Sphinx was my own son?

If you had revealed the truth, as any
human being must do, I would not have suffered   1467
  the abhorred awful shames
of my ill-fated second marriage
as a favour to the unknown hero;   1470
  Nor would I hang myself
to pay for unwitting monstrous
sins of a good loving mother and wife   1473
  in such dire throes of shame
and anguish. O Erinyes, goddesses
of vengeance! I invoke you to avenge me,   1476
  by tormenting vile Tiresias
in endless pangs of pains and throes
of agonies!

[Tiresias]

    My dear Queen Jocasta, you   1479
  have never deigned to see
me about prophecies. Even if
I had dared to volunteer to foretell, you   1482
  would have laughed at me,
as if I were a mad, blind fool.

Scene 9: *Jocasta's Testimony*

[Persephone]

Do not try to evade the critical point: 1485
   When did you, Tiresias,
hear the strange name, *Oedipus,* and
from whom for the first time?

     [Tiresias]

              About two months   1488
  before he was hailed as
our new king.

     [Third Judge]

     Who did tell you what
about Oedipus.

     [Tiresias]

      An old shepherd of King   1491
  Polybus came to see
me from Corinth.

[Fourth Judge]

Why did he come?

[Tiresias]

He wanted to ask me about his future; he   1494
 had been recently banished
from Corinth by his king.

[Fifth Judge]

       Did you
ask him why?

[Tiresias]

     He said that it was because of 1497
 the foster son of King
Polybus, called Oedipus.

[Sixth Judge]

What did he tell you about that Oedipus?   1500

[Tiresias]

He said that Oedipus
had been condemned by Apollo
such that he would kill his father and to   1503
   mate with his queen—his mother.
Hence, they banished Oedipus from
Corinth forever.

[First Judge]

                     But why did they banish   1506
the shepherd, too?

[Tiresias]

                     Because
he had brought the foundling, infant
Oedipus, rescued from Mount Cithaeron,   1509
   to the house of Polybus:
The king and queen raised Oedipus
as if he were their son and adored him   1512

as their heir to the throne
till they learnt the awful prophecy
of Apollo.

[Oedipus]

Hence, you have proved yourself,   1515
  Tiresias, that you are not
a seer of divine prophecy, at all,
but a false, sly, shameless swindler: 1518
  You pretend what you have
heard from others about things that had
already occurred as if they were your own   1521
  foreknowledge!

[Sixth Judge]

How can you
prove, Tiresias, that it was your
foreknowledge imparted to you by Apollo   1524
  as his true prophet, not
what you inferred from the reports
by the thrall of Laius and the shepherd   1527

of Polybus about the events
that had already occurred in the past?

[Tiresias]

I will speak no more. Let Apollo speak.   1530

[Apollo in disguise]

What do you want Apollo
speak for you, proud wily seer?

[Tiresias]

That Tiresias is the proven true prophet   1533
  of Apollo: I speak
only the will of my master:
I serve neither men nor women but the god.   1536

[Apollo removing his disguise]

Is that so? Then do you know
who I am?

Scene 9: *Jocasta's Testimony*

[Tiresias in awe and shock]

Who are you? Ah, Ah!
Apollo, forgive me!

*{Tiresias collapses and becomes crazy, screaming
in pains and agonies like a mad dog. The attendants
haul him out to the prison.}*

[Apollo]

How well he had played   1539
  such tragic farces to poor,
credulous, ignorant mortals,
wearing the fake mask of a sham Apollo!   1542

[Persephone]

We will bring dark things to light.

[Jocasta, kneeling]

Goddess Persephone, divine judges,
I have a woman's secret to confess!   1545

Scene 9: *Jocasta's Testimony*

[Persephone]

Reveal it, Jocasta.

[Jocasta]

The real father of Oedipus
was not Laius.

[Laius]

What, Jocasta? Then who was?   1548

[Jocasta]

Chrysippus!

[Laius]

Chrysippus?
Confess your secret intrigues,
cunning Jocasta!

[Jocasta]

Before you proposed   1551
  to my father, Menoeceus,
for our marriage, I had been deeply
in love with handsome, charming Chrysippus: 1554
  He solemnly promised
to take me as his bride to Elis
whenever he would be free to leave Thebes.   1557
  When King Pelops sent his
army, led by Chrysippus's two
half-brothers, Atreus and Thyestes, I dared   1560
  to elope with Chrysippus.

[Laius]

What? How did you scheme such a bold act?

[Jocasta]

With my motherly nurse, I waited for Chrysippus   1563
  at our usual secret
meeting place in the deep forest
outside the rampart. As he had promised,   1566

Chrysippus appeared, riding
on a swift steed, followed by two
other horsemen. Suddenly one of them   1569
   speared Chrysippus's horse,
and he tumbled down in surprise.
The other man rushed to the injured Chrysippus,   1572
   seized his sword, and plunged it
into his pounding heart. *"Well done,*
Atreus!" said one. *"His corpse should prove his*   1575
   suicide in shame for Pelops,
Thyestes," said the other.   They took
the bleeding body of Chrysippus with them.   1578
   In shock and agony, I swooned.

[Laius]

Ah, miserable Jocasta,
if you had told me the brutal fact that   1581
   Chrysippus was murdered
by vile Atreus and Thyestes,
I would have certainly informed Pelops   1584
   of his sons' horrible
crimes against their half-brother;
Even if Pelops had not believed what   1587

I would say, his misconstrued
curse would not have affected my heart
so deeply because my conscience would be free.   1590

[Jocasta]

Forgive me, my dear lord.
I was too afraid to confess my sin.

[Laius]

How deep I repent my haughty pride and greed   1593
   that caused such horrible
miseries to these innocent victims
of my sins. O divine judges, punish me   1596
   to suffer in scorching
fires till I burn into nothingness
to purge my sins. But absolve Oedipus   1599
   and Jocasta—they are
the innocent hapless victims
of my dreadful doom. Jocasta, my beloved!   1602
   Forgive me for your dire
sufferings of agony and shame.
I love you more than any who ever loved.   1605

Dear Oedipus, let me
call you my son in spirit, if not
in the flesh. I see in you noble sincerity   1608
   of man that transcends dark
tragedies wrought by the unseen
unknowable fates.

{Laius collapses and swoons. Jocasta gently
embraces him in her bosom and weeps.}

[Jocasta]

My beloved Laius,   1611
   your lofty magnanimity
redeems us from all our miseries.
Let me share with you our common fate in love.   1614

{Oedipus crawls to reach them and gently
embraces both Jocasta and Laius.}

[Oedipus]

I love you both with all
my heart and soul. May peace bless us.

[Acastus]

Behold this enigmatic man, Oedipus—   1617
   son of Chrysippus! By killing
Laius unwittingly, you have
avenged your concealed father, mocking at   1620
   my hoax-oracle in
the tragic farces of our brief life.
The stern prophecy of your parricide   1623
   has been comically
slain by the astounding confession
of your honest mother, Queen Jocasta.   1626

[Oedipus]

  Ah, dark, deep puzzles of
my origin, how subtly you perplex
my confused mind! Pretentious prophecies,   1629
   conjured up by cunning
diviners for their greed and pride,
ensnare countless credulous inane fools   1632
   to commit awful misdeeds
in trying to avert what happens
naturally in the course of our life.   1635

I am a fleeting froth
in the mystic sea of incidents:
Having sprung by mere accidents, why should   1638
   I fear to face who I am
in truth? Nothing can make me other
than who I am. Our experiences may grow   1641
   by living day by day,
but no one can foresee the unseen
yet to come!

    {Suddenly Hermes enters.}

     [Hermes]

      Pardon me in interrupting   1644
  you, again, Queen Persephone.
A piteous ghost of brave, upright, and
noble lass entreats me to guide her to see   1647
   you concerning the sacred
immutable law of heaven
in burying the dead with proper due respect.   1650

Scene 9: *Jocasta's Testimony*

[Persephone]

Welcome Hermes!   You have come
just in perfect time. Would you like
to know what astounding facts have been found   1653
   about the intriguing case
of Oedipus?

[Hermes]

Yes, of course, I do!
What did you find out about poor Oedipus,   1656
   doomed by the dire prophecy
of Apollo?

[Apollo]

What prophecy
of mine do you mean, my dear brother Hermes?   1659

[Hermes]

What? Ah, Apollo, what
are you doing here at this grim
court of the final judgment of the dead?   1662

[Apollo]

I came down to watch dire
tragic farces, conjured up by wily
mortals, dooming credulous fools with hoax   1665
  prophecies in sly abuse
of my name.

[Hermes]

What? Hoax prophecies?
Then Oedipus must be blameless for his
awful misdeeds? May I join with you to see   1668
  how such an incredible
tragic comedy unfolds in
its final climax?

[Persephone]

Certainly, Hermes!   1671
  By the way, didn't you came here
to guide a lass who had pled you
to see me about the burial rite of the dead?   1674

[Hermes]

Thank you for reminding me!
May I bring in the young lass, now?

[Persephone]

Yes. I wonder why a young maiden wants   1677
   to see me about the law
of burial.

{Hermes exits. The end of Scene #9}

Scene 10

Antigone's Sudden Appearance

Suddenly, Antigone's ghost enters, led by Hermes. She tells Oedipus that Creon put her to death as she disobeyed his stern edict not to bury her dead brother Polyneices because she believes that a proper burial of the dead is an immutable law of Heaven. The entire court pays respect to the brave upright Antigone as the champion and martyr of divine law. Jocasta revealed the astounding secret that all four children of Oedipus were born by a surrogate mother, not from her womb.

Scene 10: *Antigone's Sudden Appearance*

{Hermes brings in the ghost of Antigone.}

[Persephone to Antigone]

Who are you, gentle lass?
Why do you want to see me so urgently?   1680

[Antigone]

I am Antigone,
a daughter of King Oedipus.

[Oedipus]

What? O, my dear Antigone!   What has   1683
  brought you down to this dark
gloomy realm at the beautiful bloom
of your fresh youth?

{Antigone rushes to embrace blind Oedipus.}

[Antigone]

O my dear father, how   1686
good to see you again. Cruel
punishment, buried alive deep in
a rock-hewn cave, robbed me of my young life.   1689

[Oedipus]

What, my dear child? Who did dare
to inflict such horrible misdeeds
to you?

[Antigone]

Creon.

[Oedipus]

Creon? Your uncle?   1692

[Antigone]

Yes!

[Oedipus]

Why?

[Antigone]

Because I paid
a proper funeral rite for
Polyneices.

[Jocasta]

What? Is your brother also dead?   1695

{Antigone recognizes Jocasta and rushes to embrace her.}

[Antigone]

O my dear mother, yes
he is dead; so is Eteocles, too.

[Jocasta]

Ah heavens! Why both of them died so young?   1698

[Antigone]

They killed each other in
fierce fights: Polynices attacked Thebes
with his foreign allies; Eteocles strived   1701
  to cling on to his throne.

[Persephone]

What is Creon? Why did he punish
you, Antigone, by such a cruel death?   1704

[Antigone]

He is the new king of Thebes.
Soon after he was acclaimed to
the throne, he proclaimed that he would honour   1707
  the death of Eteocles
with solemn stately funeral.
But he sternly decreed that the corpse of   1710
  Polynices must be
left unburied in the wild to be
fed by beasts and birds as he was a vile   1713

traitor to his fatherland;
Whoever would dare to bury him
should be stoned to death.

       [Persephone]

                     Despite such stern   1716
edict, you did bury
your brother?

       [Antigone]

       Yes, with love and respect
I gave him a rite of burial, all by myself.   1719

       [Persephone]

  Why did you determine
to disobey Creon's strict
forbiddance, and to choose your cruel death?   1722

[Antigone]

It was my conscience that
had urged me to do what I did;
Resolutely, I believe that proper   1725
  burial of the dead is
an immutable law of Heaven,
although I do not know whence it came from.   1728
  Yet, I know that I must
not disobey this sacred law,
lest I provoke the wrath of Heaven; nobody   1731
  can annul and override
this timeless law of Heaven by
venting his inane whims as absurd edicts.   1734

{Persephone rises from her seat, comes
to Antigone, and gently embraces her.}

[Persephone]

Dear upright Antigone,
you are a devout true martyr!
You have resolutely upheld the sacred   1737

immutable law of
Heaven, defying the mortal's
lethal edict. We honour you as our brave   1740
   champion of the divine law.

{All judges rise from their seats to pay respect to Antigone.}

       [All Judges]

We admire you, gentle maiden,
for your noble conscience and upright acts.   1743

       [Oedipus]

   Thank you, Queen Persephone
and wise judges, for your generous,
kind blessing on my beloved Antigone.   1746
   She had been so gentle
yet brave, so devout and noble
at heart; she had sacrificed her blooming   1749
   youth, guiding the blind steps
of her accursed helpless father.
Staunchly, she shared my dire miseries of harsh   1752

exile, wandering in
drenching rains and under the scorching sun,
often hungry and footsore through wild, grim   1755
   forests, begging for doles
 to nurse her blind, helpless father
for many years till I reached Colonus, at last: 1758
   the destined harbour for my rest.

[Persephone]

Why did you dare, Antigone,
to give up the comfort and safety of home   1761
   and joined with your accursed
father, banished to such utter
miseries of hapless cruel wanderings?   1764

[Antigone]

   Simply, I followed what
my heart urged me to do: care for
my father with heartfelt love from my soul.   1767
   Somehow I believe that
such loving care for family
must be an unwritten immutable   1770

law of Heaven for us
to obey, although I do not know
whence it came from to guide our conscience.   1773

[Sixth Judge]

Your loving devotion
to the sanctity of family
uplifts our spirit, noble Antigone.   1776

[First Judge]

What did your brothers do
while you suffered to take care of
their father in miseries of wanderings?   1779

[Antigone]

They vied each other to seize
the throne of Thebes.

[Jocasta]

Ah, insolent
shameless villains in the same family!   1782

What was the real cause for
their horrible double fratricide,
Antigone? Were they poor victims of   1785
  another awful oracle?

[Antigone]

No! Their tyrannical greed for
power to rule and arrogant pride brought them   1788
  down to their terrible
mutual destructions.

[Jocasta]

They had been
both such bright, brave, and upright boys while I   1791
  raised them. My horrible
death must have ruined their noble spirit.

[Antigone]

Without grudge, mother, must we bear the grave   1794

heritage of your dire
dreadful doom; your children are ill-
fated fruits of the shameful incestuous misdeed—   1797
  we have been accursed by
the gods, and ghastly abhorred by
the people! The monstrous marriage-bed   1800
  where lay the son with his
mother, begetting us; therein
we were conceived by you. We are shameful   1803
  desecrated pollutions!

[Jocasta]

Stop it, Antigone! None of you
came from my ill womb in truth. I solemnly   1806
  swear it to the gods as
well as to you.

[Antigone]

    What did you say,
mother? Tell me, again, what you really mean.   1809

[Jocasta]

I brought up all of you
as a devoted mother with love,
but none of you are fruits of my barren   1812
   womb. My lord Laius here
be my witness: I made myself
sterile after the dire agony of casting   1815
   away my firstborn baby
at his stern behest.

[Laius]

          I know it,
Jocasta; how much we suffered our bleak   1818
   despair of childlessness
due to my inane fears of Pelops's
wrong curse!

[Fourth Judge]

       I am fascinated, Jocasta,   1821
  to watch how your mystery
unfolds as I have suspected.

[Antigone]

If what you said is really true as I   1824
   eagerly hope so, dear
mother, then who is the real mother
of Oedipus's offspring? Have we been wrongly   1827
   despised as the hapless
victims, reviled by a false incest?

[Jocasta]

Yes, my dear Antigone! You are pure;   1830
   Truly free from any blemish
of an incest! Your real mother
I called as Euryganeia, but her real   1833
   name and parentage remain
still unknown to me.

[Persephone]

      Oedipus,
reveal this mysterious woman to us.   1836
   Was she your second wife
or a mistress?

Scene 10: *Antigone's Sudden Appearance*

[Oedipus]

How deeply I
wish from my heart and soul that what Jocasta   1839
   has proclaimed would be all true.
But in truth, I know nothing of such
a mysterious woman: neither had I   1842
   a second wife nor secret
mistresses.

[Antigone in despair]

Oh my good father, how
much I wished that you knew such women!   1845
   It would have redeemed all
of us from the awful disgrace
of your despised incest.

[Persephone]

Jocasta, speak the truth   1848
   to us. Does Oedipus lie,
or is it you who lie?

[*Jocasta*]

Neither
he nor I lie: I made Oedipus lie   1851
  with her on my bed
in the dark; he had never seen
Euryganeia while he was sober or   1854
  in daylight.

[*Fourth Judge*]

Reveal secrets
of your womanly intrigues.

[*Jocasta*]

One day, not long after I wedded the new   1857
  youthful king, a tender lass
came to me as a suppliant,
begging for a secret safe shelter.   1860
  Out of pity, I took
her as a clandestine refuge
in my palace, hidden from the sight of   1863

people; she worked for me
with honesty and devotion.
 I loved her as if she were my dear daughter.   1866
 One day, I confided her
my secret fear; my young husband
desired to beget our children, but my womb   1869
 had been barren. I was
afraid that King Oedipus might get
a young new wife, and discard me away from   1872
 his bed and my throne as
Queen of Thebes. When I asked Euryganeia
to serve as a surrogate mother for me,   1875
 she willingly pledged to
help me faithfully.

[Oedipus]

Resourceful
lady, Jocasta, how glad I am to find   1878
 that I was such a naïve
fool, utterly unaware of your sly
subtle womanly intrigues!

[Antigone]

              O gods,   1881
I thank thee and my wise
mother—nay, my good prudent grand-
mother, Jocasta! You had saved us from   1884
  the abhorred vile disgrace.

{Antigone embraces Jocasta in tears of joy.}

[Fourth Judge]

Where is this mother of mystery,
you call Euryganeia? Does she still live   1887
  in Thebes, Jocasta?

[Jocasta]

No! She died soon after giving
birth to her fourth child, tender Ismene.   1890

Scene 10: *Antigone's Sudden Appearance*

[Antigone sobbing]

Ah, our loving mother!
O gracious goddess of divine
mercy, I implore you to grant a humble   1893
   daughter's heartfelt prayer:
Let me see the loving face of
my real mother and be embraced in her   1896
   warm motherly bosom,
at long last. Please find her for me,
searching everywhere in your vast mystic realm.   1899

[Persephone]

Certainly, we will search
for the mysterious woman who
had brought you to the light, Antigone.   1902
   Who can be a better
witness to solve such an intriguing
mystery that enchants us? I am curious   1905
   to see your mother myself.

Scene 10: *Antigone's Sudden Appearance*

[Fourth Judge]

I will go with Jocasta to find
the real mother of Oedipus's offspring. 1908

[Antigone]

Would you please take me with you?
This will be the day of my rebirth!

[Jocasta]

My good sweet lass, Antigone, pray here 1911
that we will find your real
mother and come back with her soon.

[Oedipus]

Hold me, gentle Antigone. I tremble 1914
in awe and excitements
like a young child waiting for his long-
lost mother. May this day bless us to be 1917
reborn in pure innocence.

Scene 10: *Antigone's Sudden Appearance*

{Antigone embraces Oedipus.}

[Antigone]

Yes, my dear father, let us pray
to the gods for the blissful miracle   1920
  of our redemption from
the accursed disgrace.

*{Oedipus and Antigone kneel in prayer. Jocasta leaves
with Fourth Judge.   The end of Scene #10.}*

Scene 11

Arete's Testimony

The ghost of a veiled woman, led by Jocasta, enters. She affirms that she gave birth to all four children by Oedipus as a surrogate mother. Antigone is overjoyed to learn that she was not a product of abhorred incest. The divine court of the final judgment decides unanimously that Oedipus is innocent from his inadvertent misdeeds. Thus acquitted at last, his vision is restored. Oedipus recognizes that the surrogate mother of his children is Arete, his beloved maiden of Corinth in his youth. The court holds a closed meeting to decide on the new lots for Oedipus and Antigone.

Scene 11: *Arete's Testimony*

{The court resumes. Fourth Judge brings in Arete, her face covered in a veil, guided by Jocasta.}

[Persephone]

Are you the real
mother of Antigone?

[Arete]

Yes, I did give   1923
her birth by Oedipus.

[Persephone]

Why do you hide your face behind
the veil?

[Arete]

My queen Jocasta wishes to keep it   1926
unseen till the proper time comes.

Scene 11: *Arete's Testimony*

[Persephone]

What is your real name and parentage?

[Arete]

I shall reveal them when my veil is removed   1929
   by the hand of the proper
person.

[Persephone]

Who is such a person?

[Arete]

Oedipus!

[Persephone]

         As I guessed it. But do you know   1932
   that he cannot see your face
even after he unveils you?

{Arete humbly prostrates as a suppliant.}

[Arete]

O goddess of mercy, gracious Persephone,   1935
   I entreat you from depth
of my heart and soul to restore
his previous keen, bright sight to Oedipus!   1938

[Persephone *to all Judges*]

   The time has come for us
to decide the final judgment
on Oedipus. Speak your verdict with fair and   1941
   clear justification.

[First Judge]

My verdict is that Oedipus
is not guilty, in spite of his ghastly   1944
   misdeeds, because he had
never intended to carry out
such horrible transgressions on purpose.   1947

[Second Judge]

Oedipus is blameless;
In a tragic irony, he carried
out his terrible misdeeds in order   1950
  to avoid them resolutely.

[Third Judge]

Oedipus is not guilty; he had
been a hapless victim of hoax oracles   1953
  and unseen accidents
in the course of his turbulent life.

[Fourth Judge]

Oedipus is innocent; enduring throes   1956
  of fears and agonies, he
persisted in seeking the truth
of his accursed misdeeds, all committed   1959
  inadvertently in his
heroic efforts to avert them.

[Fifth Judge]

I judge that Oedipus is not guilty: 1962
  Despite his awful
misdeeds, I respect his courage
and honesty to find out what he had   1965
  done unintentionally.

[Sixth Judge]

Oedipus is blameless; he has
kept up his conscience in seeking the true   1968
  causes of his misdeeds,
resolutely bearing all pangs
of painful shames and throes of dire anguishes.   1971
  He shows the nobility
of human: fleeting, frail, yet thinking
froth—a miracle in the vast sea of being.   1974

[Persephone]

  I concur with all what
you have spoken. Hence, this court
solemnly proclaims that Oedipus is   1977

innocent and free from
any blame for his inadvertent
misdeeds. Hence, I will restore him his sight.   1980

[Persephone to attendants]

Let Antigone lead in
her father, Oedipus, to us.

*{Oedipus is led in by Antigone.   Persephone rises
from her seat, comes forward, and raises Arete.}*

[Persephone]

Come Oedipus! Walk to me by yourself,   1983
as if you can see again.

*{Gently touching Oedipus's eyes, Persephone restores his
vision and his noble, handsome visage.}*

Now, gently uncover the veil
from this mysterious woman you behold.   1986

*{Trembling in awe and wonder, Oedipus tenderly
removes the veil from Arete.}*

Scene 11: *Arete's Testimony*

[Oedipus]

 O light! What a wondrous
new sight! Whom do I see here?
O gods, it is you, my dear beloved Arete!   1989

[Arete]

 O my love, Oedipus!

{Oedipus and Arete embrace in tears of joy.}

[Oedipus]

How miraculous and blissful
to see you, again, my beloved Arete!   1992
 It is your tender love
that has saved my soul, despite all
those dire fateful catastrophes in my dark,   1995
 hard, tumultuous life.

[Arete]

I have always loved you, my dear
brave Oedipus with all my heart and soul,   1998

in the secret of dark
nights during my intriguing hidden
life in Thebes as well as in the pleasant   2001
   daylight of our happy
innocent youth in our cherished
beautiful Corinth.

{Antigone rushes to Arete: they embrace
each other.}
                    O my darling daughter,   2004
  Antigone!
        [Antigone]

           Oh, dear
mother, mine! This is the day of
my rebirth nestling in your warm bosom!   2007
  It seems just a dream, too
good to believe that this is real.
How happy I am, my true dear mother,   2010
  to behold you at long last!

        [Arete]

I have missed you, my sweet tender
Antigone, so deep in my yearning heart.   2013

But I wonder why you
have come down here at the beautiful
bloom of your lovely youth, my dear Antigone?   2016

[Antigone]

Just to see you, my mother—
you are my very life, nothing else
I will ever need!

{Oedipus gently embraces Antigone.}

[Oedipus]

How wondrous to see   2019
your lovely noble face again,
my gentle Antigone.   Oh, this
ineffable bliss through long throes of dire   2022
agonies! Time in its mystic
fathomless course brings all to light,
then buries them again into boundless depths   2025
beyond fleeting memories
of all mortals.

Scene 11: *Arete's Testimony*

{Jocasta embraces Arete, Antigone, and Oedipus.}

[Jocasta]

O my beloved
children, blessed with pure, gentle, noble hearts!   2028
  I exalt the gods for
your glorious resurrection!
Gracious Goddess, Persephone, may I   2031
  bring in Laius here to
share with him this blissful miracle?

[Persephone]

Certainly, good Jocasta! Bring in Acastus   2034
  too, to see his long-lost
daughter, Arete, here.

[Jocasta]

Thank you,
goddess of mercy! Your compassion has   2037
  revived us all in bliss.

Scene 11: *Arete's Testimony*

{Jocasta leaves with attendants. Soon she returns, holding the hands of Laius and Acastus. Suddenly, Acastus recognizes his long-lost daughter, Arete.}

[*Acastus*]

Whom do I see? O holy heavens!
Arete—my long-lost beloved daughter!   2040

{Acastus swoons. Arete rushes to hold him in her arm. Soon Acastus regains his sense.}

[*Arete*]

O my dear good father,
please forgive your hapless daughter,
forlorn since so young in awful dire mishaps   2043
   of her wretched tragic life.

[*Acastus weeping*]

It is I who am guilty of
all your sufferings of terrible miseries.   2046

I beg you for your kind
forgiveness of your foolish, selfish
father. Thrones of many great kingdoms cannot   2049
  replace the pure lovely
smiles of my gentle, noble daughter
in this repenting heart!

[Second Judge]

                 Ah, clever and   2052
  resourceful King Acastus,
how miraculously the ghastly
tragedy of your wily hoax prophecies   2055
  comes out to end in such
a blissful comedy like this one!
It moves us in deep surprise and delight!   2058

[Persephone]

I hereby proclaim that
Oedipus has been found to be
innocent and blameless for his inadvertent   2061
  misdeeds by the unanimous
judgments of this final court.
You are completely free, upright Oedipus!   2064

{Oedipus kneels in humble prayer.}

[Oedipus]

Thank you, compassionate
goddess Persephone and wise judges
for your kind and fair judgment on my case!   2067
    I am very grateful that
the god of guidance, Hermes, kindly
led my blind steps to reach here and the god   2070
    of prophecy, Apollo,
came down to witness my trial.
Most of all, I am deeply inspired by   2073
    the wisdom of Apollo:
He has enlightened me to see
the sublime light of true divine justice.   2076
    I shall follow the light
of heartfelt conscience that leads us
to the way to the truth; I shall listen to   2079
    its deep inner voice, and
obey it devoutly to guide me.

[Jocasta]

Merciful goddess Persephone, I wish   2082
  to plead you for one more
gracious favour.

[Persephone]

What is it, Jocasta?

[Jocasta]

Please marry this loving pair: Oedipus to   2085
  Arete.

[Acastus]

I plead you
to unite them ever in love.

[Laius]

May their noble hearts be blessed in sacred   2088
  happy marriage, I implore.

[Persephone]

I appreciate that you wish me
to wed them. But marriage is beyond   2091
  my jurisdiction. You must
pray to Zeus and Hera for
their blessing of the long-delayed marriage   2094
  between Oedipus acquitted
and Arete found. Now, we should
decide the future lots of Oedipus and   2097
  Antigone in our realm.
As it is a confidential matter
of this court, I dismiss you to wait outside   2100
  till we make a final
decision.   I thank you, Apollo
and Hermes, for your invaluable help   2103
  in solving the enigma
of Oedipus.   As his case has been
successfully closed, you would be happy   2106
  to ascend back to your lofty
Olympus.

Scene 11: *Arete's Testimony*

[Hermes]

May I wait outside?
I am anxious to hear what you would decide   2109
  on their lots in your realm.

[Apollo]

I am very curious about it, too.

[Persephone]

Certainly, kind gods, if you do not mind it.   2112

*{While Persephone holds a confidential meeting
with the judges inside, Apollo and Hermes leave
the court to wait outside with the mortal crowds.
The end of Scene #11.}*

Scene 12

Apollo and Hermes converse on Humanity and Divinity

<Scene 12> While waiting outside the court, Apollo and Hermes pursue deep ontological discussions about the nature of humankind, their use of language, and their strange, enigmatic, and fanatic zeal in playing their fantastic and tragic comedies, called religions.

{Apollo and Hermes converse with each other
in private, separated from the mortal crowds
in the outside of the court.}

[Apollo to Hermes in private]

I am deeply moved by
the fascinating actual lives
of these mortals so vividly re-enacted   2115
   during the final judgment.
There are many things, I think, we gods
should learn from these suffering earnest humans.   2118

[Hermes to Apollo in private]

Somehow I feel the same way
as you have expressed, Apollo.
But I am not quite sure what things of these   2121
   humans have moved us so.
Would you please expound them for me?

[Apollo to Hermes in private]

The heroic bearings of their dire fates,   2124
   regardless of whether
they were real or fake, and their kind
sacrifices for others move me deeply.   2127
   Most of all, I respect
the nobility of their pure
conscience for righteousness, their heartfelt   2130
  repentance, and eager
forgiveness. A man of conscience
seeks to know who he is in truth as if   2133
  it is the ultimate
wisdom coming from *Apollo.*
And yet such a man makes me to wonder   2136
  who I really am in truth
behind this mask of *Apollo.*

     [Hermes to Apollo in private]

Yes, I concur with what you have clarified   2139
  so explicitly. I
agree that we, gods, need to learn
from the noble sufferings of these keenly   2142
  self-conscious good humans.

I confess that often I feel
deeply confused who I am. Why must I   2145
   do what I've been so used
to do: endless journeying without
rests across countless boundaries between   2148
   the heaven of immortals
 and the earth of mortals, traversing
abysmal gulfs between the realm of the quick   2151
   and the dark realm of the dead?
I must carry out all these hard and
heartbreaking tasks without exerting my own   2154
   free-will to make decisions.
I am merely a babbler
of what others say: a blind guide for the blind   2157
   alive or dead. Am I not
a witness, helpless slave of Zeus?
Enlighten me, wise brother Apollo: 2160
   How can I free myself
from this plight of my condemned godhead?

    [Apollo to Hermes in private]

Everyone must play one's role faithfully   2163

in diverse plays, conjured up
by human minds.

[Hermes to Apollo in private]

What do you mean?
Are we merely puppets, playing on the stage   2166
    set up by the humans' whims?

[Apollo to Hermes in private]

Yes. In fact, *'gods'* do not exist
in themselves but only in the impulsive   2169
    fanciful imaginations
of the fickle, fleeting humans!

[Hermes to Apollo in private]

How can what you have said be true? If you   2172
    really do not exist
in yourself, Apollo, how can you
speak on such profound mystery of non-being   2175
    of immortal beings?

[Apollo to Hermes in private]

That is how humans imagine
their unseen gods to be: all their gods are   2178
   bound to use the human
language as we are speaking now.
Their gods must think, feel, and act, as if we   2181
   were their idol-puppets,
worshiped by humans with their crazy
rituals in their weird plays, called *'religions.'*   2184

[Hermes to Apollo in private]

How such dull, frail, paltry,
fleeting creatures as humans could
make us up—powerful immortal beings—   2187
   as if we were merely
their idol-puppets?

[Apollo to Hermes in private]

By the use of
their language, the humans create the whole   2190
   world with words in their minds.

They speak of real things as well as
what they merely imagine as if those were   2193
   all true such as their *'gods'*
'souls,' *'right,'* or *'wrong:'* this is the very
mystery that puzzles me in deep amazement.   2196
   There are myriad diverse kinds
of creatures that have roamed on Earth;
But none of them had the magic ability   2199
   to use language until
the humans evolved from other
creatures. But how they acquired the subtle art   2202
   of using language, I do not know.
At birth, no human babe knows any language.
And yet, all of them somehow acquire soon   2205
   the marvellous ability
to speak a particular language
used in their society; furthermore, the humans   2208
   have invented writings
to preserve expressions of their thoughts
and feelings across the vast gulf of distances   2211
   through deep abyss of time.

[Hermes to Apollo in private]

But what is a human language?
Isn't it merely puffing sounds fading in the air?   2214
  What meaning and power
can it have for those who know nothing
of their strange noises or wriggling markings?   2217

[Apollo to Hermes in private]

  A human language is
nothing but an arbitrary
convention adhered by a society   2220
  of human beings as
their particular method used
for their social communications.   2223
  It has no absolute
meaning in itself but only for
its users.

[Hermes to Apollo in private]

  If so, how can the helpless   2226

weak humans outwit the wise,
mighty gods by using their language
that cannot convey any meaning to the divine?   2229

[*Apollo* to *Hermes in private*]

Clever priests and glib poets
pretend that their gods and goddesses
use their language as if we were members   2232
  of their own society.
Human's wily false attribution
of the mystic dubious oracles to   2235
  an *'Apollo'* is a good
example, pertinent to this play.
They choose certain women as their prophetic   2238
  priestesses who are supposed
to communicate with *'Apollo'*
while they have been induced to fall into   2241
  hallucination, mounted on
their tripod seats in deep, solemn crypts.
Whatever the priestesses say during their   2244
  delirium is deemed by
the attending priests to be the divine
words from Zeus conveyed to her via *'Apollo!'*   2247

[Hermes to Apollo in private]

How, in fact, do those priestesses
communicate with you while their mad
minds wander in their lunatic delirium?   2250

[Apollo to Hermes in private]

Absolutely, I have
nothing to do with them! Whatever
humans say about divine prophecy are   2253
  all glib fibs, conjured up
by cunning humans; they misuse
their phony gods as their idol-puppets.   2256
  Humans enjoy to play
their idiotic, absurd, tragic farces
of religions, as if they had transcended   2259
  their inane humanness
to become a *'super-god'* who
makes up all other gods to play in their   2262
  plays, called *'religions'*— all
conjured up by the wily humans.

Scene 12: *Conversing on Humanity and Divinity*

[Hermes to Apollo in private]

How can I quit from playing such a god   2265
  in their play?   I want to be
a good human!

[Apollo to Hermes in private]

             What? Why do you
want to be a helpless mortal creature?   2268

[Hermes to Apollo in private]

  I have fallen deeply
in love with a gracious, upright,
and compassionate human.

[Apollo to Hermes in private]

                 Who is she?   2271

{Suddenly Third Judge comes out the court.}

Scene 12: *Conversing on Humanity and Divinity*

[Third Judge]

Queen Persephone calls you
all to come back into the court.

*{Everyone returns to the inside of the court.
The end of Scene #12}*

Scene 13

Antigone Acclaimed as a New Divine Judge

<Scene 13> The divine court proclaims that Antigone is elected to be a new divine judge for the final judgment, and that Oedipus to be the guardian of Elysium. Apollo invites all characters involved in Oedipus's trial to come up to Olympus and present their human tragedy to move the gods. But Oedipus confesses that he cannot enact his awful past in a play. He pleads to be free as a nobody in peace, and exits the stage to vanish into the void. Hermes and Apollo follow him to watch what happens.

<Apollo and Hermes sit with the judges. Others stand
in the court. Persephone rises from her seat.}

[Persephone]

Thank you all for waiting. I hereby   2274
   solemnly proclaim that
Antigone has been elected
as our new divine judge for the final judgment   2277
   of the dead by the unanimous
acclamation of this court. Come here,
Judge Antigone, take your sacred seat   2280
   next to me!

{Stunned in awe and wonder everyone humbly
 prostrates down. In delight Hermes gently raises up
Antigone and walks affectionately with her to Persephone.
Antigone kneels in graceful devout poise.}

[Antigone in humble prostration]

Gracious Queen
Persephone and wise judges
of this divine court! Your kind trust on this   2283

humble maiden takes her
breath away. Please guide her to learn
the way of divine justice with your great wisdom   2286
    and kind generosity.
She shall strive to fulfill her sacred
duty with utmost devotion, faithfulness,   2289
    and pure conscience.

*{Persephone raises Antigone and gently puts her
on her seat as a new divine judge.}*

[Persephone]

Now, let
us celebrate this glorious
apotheosis of our new divine judge,   2292
    virtuous Antigone!

*{Persephone bestows a divine diadem and robe
upon Antigone. Everyone exults the miraculous
blissful events, elated in wonder and thanks.}*

[Apollo *to Persephone*]

I wish to know what you have
decided about a lot of new life for Oedipus.   2295

[Persephone]

Our court of the final
judgement decided to recommend
the acquitted Oedipus to King Hades   2298
    for an appointment to
be the guardian of Elysium.

{Everyone rejoices and congratulates Oedipus.}

[Apollo in delight]

Hear me, good people, what my heart urges to   2301
    speak: I want to invite
you all to visit Hermes and me
in Olympus. I request you to re-enact   2304
    your real lives on the stage
for the Olympian gods to watch,
and appreciate them; the gods have, I think,   2307
    a lot to learn from how
nobly you have endured your dire fates.
I will compose the music to go with   2310

your performance. If you
succeed in moving the deities
to weep in sympathy for you, then they   2313
   will grant whatever
you pray for with divine blessing.
How does my proposal for such a playing   2316
   in Olympus sound to you?

[Laius]

O wise speaker of truth, Apollo!
We shall obey most willingly to perform   2319
   whatever you command us
to play with all our heart and soul.

[Acastus]

It would be a fantastic dream for us   2322
   to visit unseen Olympus.

[Hermes]

I will stay here to help you all
prepare for it. When I deem that you are ready   2325

for moving performance,
I will guide you to Olympus.

{Oedipus humbly kneels to supplicate.]

[Oedipus]

Please forgive me, wise Apollo and kind   2328
   Hermes.   I confess that
I cannot replay my awful past
on stage. At last, I am freed from utter   2331
   agonies and throes of stern
punishments by my conscience
as I learn the truth through my final trial   2334
   at this court. There is nothing
else I desire to attain. I wish
to forget myself in pure oblivion.   2337

[Apollo to Oedipus]

   I respect what you mean,
bold man of insightful wisdom!

{Hermes stands up, and gently raises Oedipus.}

[Hermes]

You are the bravest man of true conscience,   2340
  inspiring us to hear
deep inner voice of one's conscience!

[Oedipus, bowing to Persephone and judges]

Gracious Queen Persephone and wise judges!   2343
  Your solemn admission
of Antigone to be a new judge
of this divine court of the final judgment   2346
  is a miraculous blessing
beyond what I ever dreamed of.
I do not desire any further honour   2349
  nor vain power to rule.

[Persephone]

I understand what you intend.
You are completely free to follow what   2352
  your conscience commands.

[Oedipus to all]

It is time for me to depart.
I bid you all my farewell with deep love. 2355

[Persephone]

To where are you going?

[Oedipus]

Nowhere. I shall vanish into
nobody in deep void unknown to all. 2358

{Oedipus walks away in awesome poise.}

[Hermes]

I will follow him to see
what happens.

Scene 13: *Antigone Acclaimed as a Divine Judge*

[Apollo]

I will join with you
to witness this strange and enigmatic event!   2361

*{Hermes and Apollo exit the stage,
following Oedipus. All others remain
stunned in awe and overwhelmed in wonder.
The end of Scene 13.}*

Scene 14

Departure of Oedipus
into Nothingness

Hermes and Apollo returns to the stage. Hermes relates to Antigone how miraculously Oedipus has transcended into nobody. In the absence of the crucial protagonist, Apollo concedes that his wishful plan for the play, *Tragic Comedies of Humans,* to be presented to the gods in Olympus has to be abandoned. Then Hermes asserts resolutely that he will play the role of Oedipus. Thus encouraged, Apollo leads all witnesses to enact their past in the play in the Olympus. Hermes follows as a blind protagonist, tenderly guided by Antigone in love.

{Hermes and Apollo returns to the stage.}

　　[Antigone to Hermes]

　O God of compassion,
please share with us what actually
happened to my dear father.

　　　[Hermes]

　　　　　　　　　Certainly,　　　　　2364
　I will relate to you,
divine judge Antigone, what had
happened as much as I could perceive.　　2367
　　We followed the solitary
steps trodden by your bold, brave father,
passing through mysterious, strange passages,　　2370
　　over the vast span of lands,
past shadows of sunsets, and mystic
shores of fanciful ephemeral dreams.　　2373
　　When he reached the very end
of lands by sea, he stood still, rapt
in deep thought, gazing at the horizon.　　2376

Suddenly an ethereal
rainbow appeared in the lofty sky;
It formed a graceful numinous bridge which   2379
   connected the edge of land
to the boundless sky. Your father
humbly prostrated on earth in solemn prayer.   2382
   Then he took off the ground,
and began to climb up the rainbow.
In awesome stately grandeur, he ascended   2385
   high and miraculously
transcended into the deep void.

[Antigone]

Did he reach the Olympus by himself   2388
   without your divine guidance?

[Hermes]

He did not come to the Olympus,
I am certain. But whereto he disappeared   2391
   I do not know at all.

Scene 14: *Departure of Oedipus into Nothingness*

[Persephone]

What a strange, enigmatic, and
mysterious end we hear! Apollo,   2394
   do you confirm it? If so,
would you please explain to us how
such bewildering events could happen?   2397

[Apollo]

   I saw what had happened
as Hermes related vividly.
Everything changes from being to non-being,   2400
   then back to being, and so on
in the cosmic drama of nature.

[Persephone]

Do you still hope to stage your proposed play   2403
   by these humans without its main
protagonist to show it to the gods
in Olympus? If you do not, I will dismiss   2406
   them to return to their allotted
provenances as soon as possible.

Scene 14: *Departure of Oedipus into Nothingness*

[Apollo in sombre mood]

Sincerely, I believe that it would be   2409
   a meaningful as well as
deeply moving play if its bold
protagonist had agreed to perform   2412
   his crucial tragic role.
Since he refused it and vanished
forever into nothingness, I have to   2415
   abandon my wishful plan
of the play.

[Hermes in pensive mood]

      Apollo, if you
find someone to play the role of Oedipus,   2418
   would you carry out your plan?

[Apollo]

My dear brother Hermes, I don't know
where I could find such a brave, sincere person.   2421

[Hermes]

Right here and now; I will
assume the role of Oedipus
as best as I can!

[Apollo]

What? You, immortal god,   2424
willing to play as if
you were a helpless mortal creature?

[Hermes]

Yes, my wise brother Apollo. I am   2427
determined to do it
as it is the best and only way
to learn the deep mystery of human beings.   2430

[Apollo to Hermes]

Thank you, my trusty brother.
You will be the perfect protagonist!

Scene 14: *Departure of Oedipus into Nothingness*

[Apollo to all]

I will lead you all up to the Olympus   2433
   to perform *'Tragic Comedies*
of Humans.'

{Apollo guides all witnesses to Olympus:
Laius and Jocasta hand in hand follow him;
Next, Acastus and Arete follow them;
Tiresias and the Thrall walk behind.}

[Hermes to Antigone]

I am blind; Hold my hand;
Guide me through this mystic inner journey   2436
   to see the light, my beloved
Antigone!

[Antigone]

I will obey you
ever in love, my revered compassionate Hermes.   2439

{Tenderly Antigone holds Hermes's hand;
They walk together in love off the stage.}

The End

Epilogue

The present play on the mythological character, Oedipus, was inspired by and based on the Theban tragedies of Sophocles (c. 497 – c. 405): *Antigone; Oedipus Tyrannus;* and *Oedipus at Colonus.* It unfolds an imaginary trial of Oedipus in the divine court of the final judgment in Hades, following the self-blinded tragic hero Oedipus met his death at Colonus in awe-inspiring dignity.

[1]   The conversations of the Theban characters portrayed in this drama have been based on the classic texts of the Theban tragedies of Sophocles (496 – 406 BCE): *Oedipus the king, Oedipus at Colonus,* and *Antigone;* translated by Francis Storr (1912), Loeb Classical Library, Harvard University Press.

[2]   The imaginary judgement of the dead in Hades was conjured up from *The Odyssey* of Homer [Books 11 and 24], translated by A. T. Murray (1919), Loeb Classical Library, *The Republic* of Plato [Book 10], translated by P. Shorey, Loeb Classical Library (1935), *The Aeneid* of Virgil [Book 6], translated by H.R. Fairclough, Loeb Classical Library (1916), and *The Divine Comedy* of Dante, translated by C.S. Singleton (1970-80), Princeton University Press.

[3]   The plausible affairs among Laius, Chrysippus, and Pelops {lines 798 – 969 in Scene #7 } were speculated from the relevant legends cited in *Early Greek Myth* by Timothy Ganz (1993), Johns Hopkins University Press.

[4]   The alleged love affairs between Chrysippus and Jocasta {lines 1549 – 1644 in Scene # 9} are merely a fictitious invention by the author.

[5]   The character 'Acastus' of Corinth {lines 484 – 637 in Scene #5} was conjured up to make the enigmatic legend of Oedipus sensible to the best of this author's imagination. It is purely a fictional character who plays a critical role only in this play.

[6] The character 'Arete' {lines 1794 – 1922 in Scene #10 and lines 1923 – 2080 in Scene #11} was invented to be the Acastus's graceful daughter, who had been deeply in love with Oedipus in their happy youth in Corinth, and to serve as the secret surrogate mother of all four children by Oedipus in Thebes. This is purely a fanciful invention imagined by the author; there are no legends in Greek myth that may allude to it.

[7] The imaginary dialogues between Apollo and Hermes on the nature of humankind, their use of language, and their invention of religions {lines 2123 – 2217 in Scene #12} are merely the author's private invention; they have nothing to do with the traditional thoughts of the Greek mythology or the beliefs of the Greek religion.

[8]   The election of Antigone to be a judge of the divine court of the final judgment {lines 2274 – 2293 in Scene #13} is merely a wishful invention.

[9]   The Apollo's invitation of all characters to re-enact their lives in a play, *"Tragic Comedies of Humans,"* to be performed in the Olympus for the gods to watch and appreciate {lines 2301 – 2327 in Scene #13}; the Oedipus's polite decline and his awe-inspiring sublime transcendence into nothingness at peace {lines 2328 – 2402 in Scene #13}, and Hermes's offer to assume the crucial role of Oedipus to perform the play {lines 2403 – 2439 in Scene #14} are purely the author's private imaginations in which he wishes to conclude this play beyond the enigmatic ancient Greek legend of the awe-inspiring mythical character: *Oedipus.*

Art Aeon

Made in the USA
Coppell, TX
23 December 2020

0132